THE OFFICIAL
COOKBOOK

The WIZARD of Oz™

THE OFFICIAL
COOKBOOK

Recipes **by** Elizabeth Fish & Elena P. Craig
Written **by** Emma Carlson Berne

INSIGHT
EDITIONS

SAN RAFAEL · LOS ANGELES · LONDON

Contents

CHAPTER 4:

The Wicked Castle

CHAPTER 5:

Emerald City

Introduction

The Land of Oz glitters in our imaginations, forever Technicolor yellow, green, red, and blue. Since the first moment the gray Kansas barnyard flashed on movie screens in 1939, we've never really left Dorothy, Toto, and her friends. Her world is still within us, with angry trees pitching bright red apples, the Lollipop Guild dancing and scowling, the Tin Man rusting up and needing a little squirt from his oil can.

Even though we can't reach through the screen and grab one of those delicious lollipops for ourselves, in front of our own stoves, we can bring the Land of Oz a little closer to home. These recipes will lead you along Dorothy's own path, from Auntie Em's farm kitchen, filled with homey goodies, into rainbow-drenched Munchkinland, where you can choose between Blueberry Basil Marshmallow Bluebirds (page 73) and Glinda Strawberry Jasmine Bubble Tea (page 67).

Travel with Dorothy down the yellow brick road and you'll find an Apple Shrub Mocktini (page 95, good for using with those bruised apples after they hit the ground), you can pay homage to our favorite road buddies with I'm Feeling Chicken Liver Pâté (page 107) and If I Only Had a Heart-Shaped Ravioli (page 98), and in the witch's castle, stir up some Wicked Lemonade (page 121) and offer it along with an Emerald City Quiche (page 145).

Sweet, savory, and flavory, these recipes are perfect for your *The Wizard of Oz* viewing party, or for a quiet night at home with you and your very own Cowardly Lion (*rawr!*). Turn these pages, pull back the curtain on the Wizard of Oz, and bring some of his magic into your kitchen—where the only surprise will be just how delicious these dishes are.

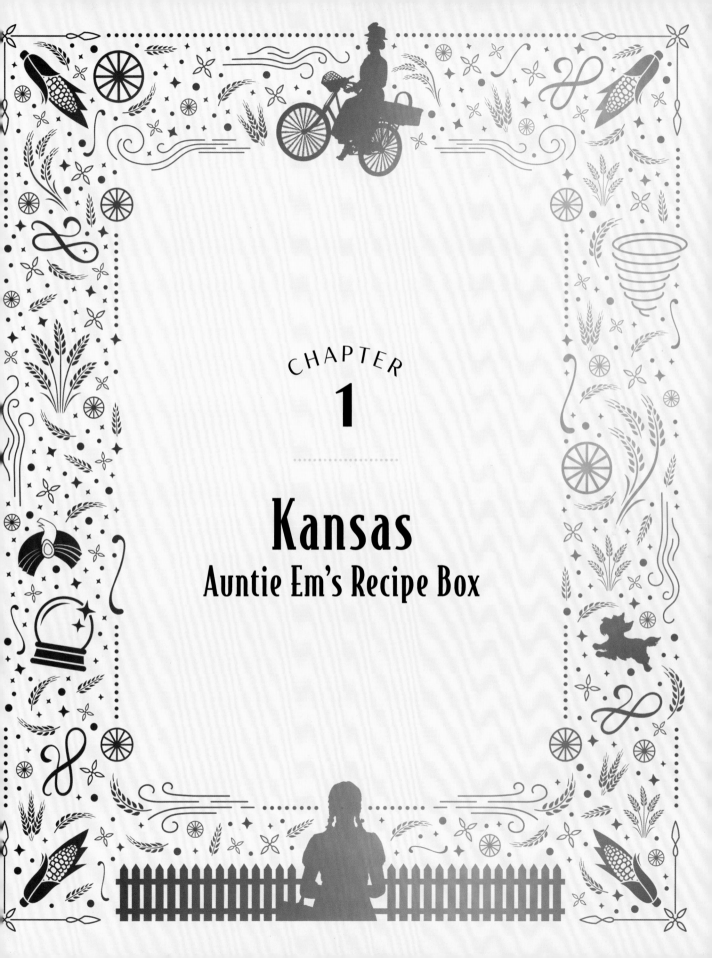

CHAPTER

1

Kansas
Auntie Em's Recipe Box

Auntie Em's Crullers

Yield: About 12 crullers | V

"Can't work on an empty stomach," Auntie Em tells Hunk, Zeke, and Hickory before offering up a plate of her delicious maple-glazed crullers, which they gratefully help themselves to. Still, your own farmhands don't have to be heading off for a day of manual labor under the Kansas sun to enjoy these deep-fried delicacies. Make the dough for the crullers the day before but fry them up as close to serving time as possible.

FOR THE CRULLERS:

1½ cups all-purpose flour

½ cup milk

½ cup water

4 ounces unsalted butter, cut into cubes (any temperature)

3 tablespoons sugar

½ teaspoon salt

4 large eggs, divided

6 cups vegetable oil, for frying

FOR THE MAPLE GLAZE:

1 cup powdered sugar

3 tablespoons maple syrup

Up to 1 teaspoon milk, heavy cream, plant-based milk, or water

SPECIALTY TOOLS:

Parchment paper

Pastry bag with a large star tip

TO MAKE THE CRULLERS: Using a fine-mesh strainer or a sifter, sift the flour over a large bowl and set aside. Place the milk, water, butter, sugar, and salt into a medium, heavy-bottomed saucepan. Bring to a boil over medium heat, stirring constantly, using a wooden spoon or a rubber spatula. Turn off the heat immediately when the milk comes to a boil and add the flour. Stir vigorously until well combined. When all of the flour has been absorbed, place over medium heat and stir constantly for about 2 minutes, or until the dough pulls away from the sides and is smooth. Transfer the dough into a large bowl and set aside until it is just warm to the touch, about 15 minutes (set your timer). Using a fork, beat one of the eggs in a small bowl. Add the egg into the bowl with the dough and mix until thoroughly incorporated. Repeat with 2 more eggs. Beat the last egg and add in as little as possible, until the dough just begins to become runny and is no longer clinging to your spoon. Place a piece of plastic wrap directly on the surface of the dough and refrigerate for at least 1 hour but up to 24 hours.

While the dough is chilling, cut parchment paper into fifteen 4-inch squares. Using a round glass or cutter, draw a 2½- to 3-inch circle in the middle of one of the squares to use as a template. Using a rubber spatula, place some of the dough into the pastry bag, filling it no more than two-thirds of the way full. Place another square over the template and use your traced circle as your guide to evenly pipe the dough while overlapping the ends. Repeat until you have used up all the dough, refilling the pastry bag as needed. Let the crullers sit, uncovered, while you heat the oil.

Line a baking sheet with paper towels and place a wire cooling rack on the paper towels. Pour the oil into a deep, heavy-bottomed pot or Dutch oven until it is about 3 inches deep. Heat the oil until it reaches 375°F. Gently pick up one cruller-topped parchment square and place it carefully, face down, into the hot oil with the paper still attached. Once it detaches itself, after about 10 seconds, remove the paper with tongs. Allow the cruller to continue frying until slightly puffed and cooked through, about 2 minutes on each side, using tongs to gently turn it. Transfer to the wire rack to drain off any residual oil. Working with one square at a time, continue by adding up to two or three crullers to the oil, depending on your comfort level and the size of the pot.

TO MAKE THE MAPLE GLAZE: In a small bowl, stir the powdered sugar with the maple syrup until smooth. Drizzle in a few drops of milk or other liquid at a time, stirring between additions, until the glaze is smooth and just starting to drip off the spoon.

TO GLAZE THE CRULLERS: Dip the slightly warm or room-temperature crullers into the glaze. Place back on the wire rack, glazed-side up. Continue with the remaining crullers. Serve immediately if possible, or the same day.

Always on Hand Cake

Yield: 8 servings | V

There isn't time for fancy cooking on a farm, which is why Auntie Em's simple cake has only three ingredients—flour, sugar, and eggs. Whip the batter thoroughly to incorporate air, then fold in lemon zest and juice for lemon cake or make a flourless chocolate version by replacing the flour with cocoa powder for chocolate cake. Leave it plain and top it with strawberries or add a snowfall of powdered sugar. Any way you prepare it leaves curious nieces like Dorothy begging for seconds.

Butter or oil, for greasing

4 large eggs, room temperature

1 cup sugar

1 cup flour, divided

2 tablespoons powdered sugar (optional)

TO SERVE:

Over the Rainbow Crepe Cake filling (page 41) or 2 cups of heavy cream, whipped (optional)

1 pint fresh strawberries, sliced (optional)

Preheat the oven to 300°F. Grease the interior of an 8- or 9-inch springform pan. Cut a circle of parchment paper to line the bottom of the pan.

In a large mixing bowl or the bowl of a stand mixer, add the eggs and sugar. Using a hand beater or the whisk attachment, begin mixing on low speed. Gradually increase the speed to high and mix for 6 to 8 minutes. The batter should be thick, very pale yellow, and leave a ribbon when you lift the whisk or beaters. If using a stand mixer, remove the bowl. Using a fine-mesh strainer or a sifter, sift ½ cup of flour directly into the bowl. Use a rubber spatula to fold in the flour. Repeat with another ½ cup of flour. Turning the bowl slightly and often in the same direction, keep folding until all the flour has been just absorbed. Do not overmix.

Pour the batter into the prepared pan. Place it into the oven and raise the temperature to 350°F. Raising the temperature is important so set yourself a reminder if needed. Bake for 30 to 35 minutes, or until the cake is lightly golden brown and has formed a solid crust on top.

Cool the cake completely before removing the sides of the pan. Dust evenly with the powdered sugar, if using, and serve, if desired, with fresh strawberries and Over the Rainbow Crepe Cake filling or whipped cream.

SIMPLY DELICIOUS VARIATIONS

STRAWBERRY SHORTCAKE: Make the Always on Hand Cake the day beforehand and store it in an airtight container, having allowed it to cool completely. Follow the recipe for the Over the Rainbow Crepe Cake filling (page 41). Slice the cake in half horizontally through the middle and toast it for about 7 to 10 minutes in the oven, or until it just starts to become crispy and brown slightly. Allow to cool slightly and spread two-thirds of the filling over the bottom layer. Arrange about a pint of sliced strawberries over the filling and top with the other half of the cake, cut-side down. Ice the top of the cake with the remaining filling and decorate with another pint of sliced strawberries, if desired.

LEMON: Add ¼ cup of lemon juice and 1 tablespoon of lemon zest before adding the flour to make a Simply Delicious Lemon Cake. Serve with fresh raspberries and/or the lemon curd from the Cake Truffle Eggs (page 20).

CHOCOLATE (GF): Use 1 cup of high-fat (20 to 24 percent) Dutch-process cocoa powder in place of the flour for a light, rich flourless chocolate cake.

Dinner on the Farm Rolls

Yield: 32 rolls | V

Classic cooks like Auntie Em can use this preparation for soft, tender rolls—thanks to the flour slurry added to the dough. As the yeasty aroma fills your kitchen, imagine yourself already spreading butter on these warm rolls. This same dough is also the secret to Auntie Em's Prize-Winning Pulled Pork Cinnamon Rolls (page 16).

2 cups whole milk, divided

5 tablespoons water

5 to 6 cups all-purpose flour, or more as needed, divided

⅓ cup granulated sugar

2 teaspoons kosher salt, or 1 teaspoon fine salt

1½ tablespoons instant yeast (2 standard packets)

⅔ cup unsalted butter, room temperature, divided

2 large eggs, room temperature

Oil, for greasing

SPECIALTY TOOLS:

Kitchen thermometer

NOTE

If you would like to make the dough a day in advance, divide the dough in half and place each piece into a well-oiled resealable gallon-size bag. Remove as much air as you can as you seal the bag closed. Refrigerate for up to 24 hours before shaping into rolls.

Measure the milk into a microwave-safe 1-quart measuring cup or medium-size bowl. Spoon 5 tablespoons of the measured milk and the water into a small saucepan. Add 4 teaspoons of the flour. Whisk constantly over medium heat until the mixture thickens, making distinct lines in the paste. Take the slurry off the heat and set it aside to cool to room temperature.

In a large bowl, combine 4 cups of the flour, the sugar, salt, and yeast. Whisk until combined (no need to clean the whisk between procedures). Heat the remaining milk until warm, about 110°F. Whisk half of the butter (6 tablespoons) and the eggs into the cooled flour paste. Whisk in the warm milk until well combined.

Using the rubber spatula to stir, slowly add the milk mixture into the flour-sugar mixture. Fold until the flour has been incorporated. Cover with plastic wrap or a tea towel and allow to sit at room temperature for 20 minutes. Uncover and, using a rubber spatula, continue sprinkling in ½ cup flour, a little at a time, folding in the flour completely.

Turn the dough onto a floured surface. Sprinkle ¼ cup of flour over the dough and turn it over. Sprinkle the other side with another ¼ cup and begin kneading with your hands, sprinkling on more flour as needed, until the dough is smooth and still slightly tacky. Lightly grease a large bowl with oil. Place the dough in the bowl, turning it to coat it with the oil. Cover the bowl with an oiled piece of plastic wrap (see note). Place in a warm, draft-free area and let rise until doubled. The time this takes varies greatly, depending on the temperature of your kitchen, taking anywhere from 45 to 90 minutes. It helps to set a timer for 15-minute intervals after the first 45 minutes so you can check on how the dough is rising.

Using about half of the reserved butter, grease a rimmed 9-by-13-inch baking dish or two 8-inch square or round cake pans.

Turn the dough out onto a work surface. Cut the dough into equal 32 pieces. Shape each piece into a smooth ball by tucking the ends around themselves and pinching the seams together. Place the seam-side down into your prepared baking pan, spacing them into even rows, about a ½-inch apart. Cover the rolls with oiled plastic wrap and let rise for an additional 30 to 60 minutes, or until the rolls have doubled in size.

Meanwhile, preheat the oven to 375°F. Bake the rolls for 18 to 21 minutes, until golden brown. Remove the rolls from the oven. Melt the remaining reserved butter and brush the tops of the rolls gently with a pastry brush or crumpled paper towel.

Auntie Em's Prize-Winning Pulled Pork Cinnamon Roll

Yield: 9 rolls

Auntie Em doesn't need to fire up her wood stove for this recipe—and neither do you. This sweet-savory combination might look complicated, but it's made almost entirely with leftovers: Pull Me Out of the Pen Pork (page 27) and Dinner on the Farm Rolls (page 15) dough, rolled up with a creamy maple glaze drizzled over the top. Serve to the hungry farmhands in your house and let visions of county-fair blue ribbons sweep you away like a twister.

FOR THE PORK CINNAMON BUNS:

Flour, for dusting

½ recipe Dinner on the Farm Rolls (page 15), continuing as below after the first rise (see note)

1½ cups Pull Me Out of the Pen Pork (page 27), room temperature

½ tablespoon cinnamon

3 tablespoons brown sugar

½ cup water

Butter or oil, for greasing

FOR THE MAPLE GLAZE:

1 cup powdered sugar

3 tablespoons maple syrup

1 teaspoon milk, divided

NOTE

Make a double batch (one whole dough recipe) or use the other half to make Dinner on the Farm Rolls or the Festive Munchkin Goodwitches (page 61). The dough can be refrigerated overnight and the rolls made the next day, skipping the first double rise. Allow for a longer final rise, about 60 to 90 minutes.

TO MAKE THE PORK CINNAMON BUNS: Generously butter or oil an 8- or 9-inch square or round pan.

After the first double rise (or straight from the refrigerator, see recipe) transfer the Dinner on the Farm Rolls dough to an evenly floured surface. Using a well-floured rolling pin, roll the dough out into an 18-by-12-inch rectangle. In a small bowl, combine the cinnamon and brown sugar. Pour the water into another small bowl. Sprinkle half of the cinnamon mixture over half of the dough. Fold the other half over the sugar mixture. Repeat by sprinkling half of the remaining cinnamon sugar over half the dough and again folding the remaining half over. Flour the rolling pin well and roll the dough back into an 18-by-12-inch rectangle. Starting with the long side closest to you, 1 inch in, spread the pork lengthwise evenly over two-thirds of the dough, pressing down on the pork. Wet the remaining dough along the long edge farthest from you with water. Tightly roll the dough from the pork end toward the wet edge, finishing with the seam down. Cut about ½ inch off both ends to make sure the filling is even for each roll. Using a sharp knife, cut into nine even pieces. Place the rolls flat into the prepared pan and sprinkle with the remaining cinnamon sugar. Cover with a greased piece of plastic wrap and let rise until doubled (see note).

Preheat the oven to 350°F. Remove the plastic wrap and bake the rolls for 25 to 30 minutes, or until lightly golden brown. Remove from the oven and set on a cooling rack for 15 minutes.

TO MAKE THE MAPLE GLAZE: In a small bowl, combine the powdered sugar with the maple syrup. Drizzle in a small amount of milk at a time until you reach a smooth and thick yet stirrable paste.

If not serving from the pan, remove the buns and arrange on a serving plate. Drizzle or spread the glaze over the buns and allow it to set for another 15 minutes before serving.

Peach Iced Tea

Yield: 6 to 8 servings | GF, V, V+

Auntie Em probably wishes she'd offered some of this special-occasion refresher to Miss Gulch that day in the parlor when she came to take away poor little Toto. The peachy tea might have helped sweeten her up. Try serving this on your own porch, along with a tray of mix-ins: ginger or strawberry syrup, ginger ale or seltzer, and mint sprigs.

4 cups water, divided

3 tea bags

2 peaches, peeled and sliced, or 2 cups frozen

Up to ½ cup Cordial Munchkin Sweetness strawberry syrup (page 69) or ginger syrup (page 161) (optional)

Mint sprigs, for garnish (optional)

Up to 16 ounces of ginger ale or seltzer (optional)

Bring 2 cups of water to a boil in a small saucepan. Turn off the heat and add the tea bags. Steep for 10 minutes. Remove and discard the tea bags and add the remaining 2 cups of cold or room-temperature water. Transfer to a pitcher or jar and refrigerate for about 1 hour before continuing.

Blend the peaches and tea in a blender until smooth. Strain if you want to, but depending on your blender this step may not be necessary. The ginger or strawberry syrup can be added to taste at this point and/or offered on the side when serving. Chill for at least 2 hours or overnight. Pour over ice in a pitcher or glasses, offering the mint sprigs, syrups, and ginger ale and/or seltzer on the side, if using.

Cake Truffle Eggs

Yield: About 16 eggs; about 1 cup lemon curd | V

Perhaps over the rainbow, all the eggs are chocolaty and dipped in tangy lemon curd, but Auntie Em probably isn't going to find this treat next time she ventures into her chicken coop. Instead, you can whip up these special eggs in your own kitchen, using premade lemon curd for speed and convenience, or making your own (it's easier than it seems!). Serving suggestion? Tuck these into a checkered napkin and display them in a basket, as if they've just been plucked from under a candy hen. You'll feel just like you're on Auntie Em and Uncle Henry's farm.

FOR THE LEMON CURD:

1 tablespoon lemon zest

⅓ cup lemon juice

1 teaspoon cornstarch

⅔ cup sugar

4 egg yolks

4 tablespoons unsalted butter

⅛ teaspoon kosher salt

FOR THE CAKE POP MIX:

½ recipe Flower Pot Cupcakes (page 65; about 12 cupcakes)

4 ounces cream cheese, softened

4 tablespoons unsalted butter, softened

½ cup powdered sugar

FOR THE FILLING AND COATING:

½ cup lemon curd, homemade or store-bought

2 cups white chocolate chips

1 tablespoon coconut oil

TO MAKE THE LEMON CURD: In a small bowl, add the lemon zest to the lemon juice and set aside.

In a nonreactive, heavy-bottomed saucepan, mix the cornstarch and sugar together. Add the egg yolks all at once and whisk until the mixture is pale, 1 to 2 minutes. Add the lemon juice mixture and whisk again until incorporated. Place over medium-low heat and cook, stirring constantly until the mixture thickens, 3 to 5 minutes. Make sure to scrape the bottom and edges of the pan so none of the mixture burns.

Once the mixture is thickened, add the butter and salt and stir until all the butter has melted and is combined. Remove the pan from the heat and pass the mixture through a fine-mesh sieve into an airtight container, and refrigerate for at least 4 hours or, better yet, overnight.

TO MAKE THE CAKE POP MIX: In the bowl of a stand mixer fitted with a paddle attachment or a large mixing bowl if using a hand mixer, mix the cake until crumbly. Add the cream cheese and butter, mix on medium-high until everything is incorporated and a dough starts to form. Add the powdered sugar and mix again until fully incorporated.

Line a baking sheet with a silicone mat or parchment paper. Working with about 2 tablespoons of dough, roll it in your hands until you form a smooth ball. Using your thumb, make an indent in the ball and fill it halfway with lemon curd, about 1 teaspoon. Pinch the dough closed over the lemon curd. Gently shape the ball into an egg shape by tapering one end. Repeat with the remaining dough. Chill for 30 minutes.

At the end of the 30 minutes, remove the eggs from the refrigerator and set aside. Melt the chocolate and coconut oil in a microwave-safe bowl in 30-second bursts. Stir between each time until smooth. Dip each egg to coat, shake off the excess, and set back on the baking sheet. Allow to set for 20 to 30 minutes or chill again for 10 minutes.

Serve immediately or store in an airtight container in the refrigerator for up to 3 days.

Tried and True Pie Crust

Yield: 1 double 9-inch piecrust | V

For all the baking she's doing, Auntie Em needs a good, reliable piecrust recipe—and she happens to have the perfect one in her recipe box. Hers uses a classic combination of butter and shortening, and this flaky crust will be your workhorse for Emerald City Quiche (page 145), "She Was Hungry" Baked Apples (page 91), and of course, There's No Place Like Home(made) Apple Pie (page 167). It'll leave you and your farmhands asking for seconds—and maybe even thirds!

2½ cups all-purpose flour, plus more for dusting

2 tablespoons powdered sugar (see note if making a savory crust)

1 teaspoon salt

⅔ cup unsalted butter, very cold, divided

¼ cup solid shortening, very cold

⅓ to ½ cup ice water

NOTE

If you are using this crust recipe to make a savory pie or quiche, omit the sugar.

In a large bowl, combine the flour, powdered sugar, and salt. Cut ½ cup of the cold butter and the shortening into ¼-inch cubes. Using a pastry cutter or two forks, work the butter into the flour mixture until all of the pieces are about pea-size. Alternatively, use a food processor and briefly pulse the butter and dry ingredients together five to seven times, until pea-size, and transfer the mixture to a large mixing bowl.

Sprinkle ⅓ cup ice water over the flour mixture. Using the pastry cutter or a rubber spatula, mix until the dough just comes together, adding 1 tablespoon more water at a time as needed. Using your hand, pack the dough into a ball. Divide the dough into two pieces and flatten each piece into 1-inch-thick disks. Wrap the two disks tightly with plastic wrap and refrigerate for at least 1 hour, or up to 3 days.

Transfer one piece of the chilled dough to a well-floured surface. Using a floured rolling pin, roll out into a ⅛-inch-thick circle, about 4 inches wider than your pie plate. Fold the dough in fourths and place into the pie plate and gently unfold and press the pie dough into the bottom and sides. Trim the edges with a knife or kitchen scissors, leaving a ½-inch overhang.

If making a double-crust pie, repeat with the second piece of dough, rolling it out large enough to fill your pie pan with a ¾-inch overhang. If you are using the crust for a quiche or a crumble-topped pie, double wrap the remaining dough and refrigerate for up to 3 days or freeze for up to 2 months.

Toto Shortbread Cookies

Yield: About 32 cookies | V

Faithful little Toto is Dorothy's best friend—surely, he deserves his own spot on your table as well. You can re-create the famous cairn terrier in shortbread with just a few ingredients, plus a canine-shaped cookie cutter. Nutty brown butter adds an extra layer of flavor to these cookies that are almost too cute to eat.

1 cup unsalted butter, divided

½ cup packed light brown sugar

1 teaspoon salt, divided

2 cups all-purpose flour, plus more for rolling

1 teaspoon cinnamon

4 tablespoons sugar

SPECIALTY TOOLS:

Toto or Scottie dog cookie cutter

Add ½ cup of butter to a small saucepan over medium heat and stir until melted. Once the butter is melted, continue to cook it, stirring occasionally, until most of the butter has turned clear, the solids have browned on the bottom, and the butter has a nutty aroma. This will take 5 to 7 minutes (do not rush this with higher heat, as you will burn the butter). Once the butter is browned, remove it from the heat and transfer it to a heatproof bowl. Allow to cool for 15 minutes.

In a large bowl or stand mixer, add the remaining ½ cup of butter, the brown butter, and brown sugar. Use the paddle attachment to combine until light and fluffy. Add ½ teaspoon of salt and the flour and stir until well combined.

Remove the dough from the bowl, separate into two disks, wrap both in parchment paper, and refrigerate for 3 hours.

Using one disk at a time, roll out on a floured surface and cut out as many Toto shapes as possible, rerolling scraps as needed. Place the cutouts on one of the prepared baking sheets and refrigerate for 15 minutes. Repeat with the second disk of dough.

While the cookies are chilling, line two baking sheets with a silicone baking mat or parchment paper and preheat the oven to 350°F and mix together, in a shaker container if possible, the remaining ½ teaspoon of salt, the cinnamon, and sugar. Shake to combine.

Before putting the cookies in the oven, evenly sprinkle the cinnamon mixture over each cookie. Bake for 9 to 11 minutes, or until browning at the edges and firm. Remove from the oven and allow to cool completely before storing in an airtight container. Cookies can be stored for 5 days.

Pull Up to the Table Bacon Cheddar Biscuits

Yield: About twelve 2½-inch biscuits

Crumbly bacon and the zing from chives and extra-sharp cheddar make these flaky biscuits perfect for eating six at a time—which is just what Hunk, Zeke, and Hickory like to do after a long day on the farm. Uncle Henry has to compete if he wants to get any for himself. If Auntie Em can wrestle any away from all these hungry people before they're gone, she slices them in half to make Farmhand Egg Sandwiches (page 34).

8 slices bacon

About ¼ teaspoon freshly ground black pepper

4 to 4½ cups pastry or all-purpose flour (see notes), divided

1½ tablespoons baking powder

1 teaspoon baking soda

1½ teaspoons kosher salt

3 tablespoons sugar

1 cup shredded extra-sharp cheddar cheese

¼ cup chopped fresh chives

¾ cup unsalted butter, frozen

1½ cups cold buttermilk, plus more if needed

NOTES

Pastry flour will produce a slightly lighter biscuit because it contains a lower protein content. The size of your biscuits will determine how long to bake them for, so adjust your time a few minutes one way or the other as needed. To make ahead, freeze the biscuits for 1 hour on the tray and then transfer them into resealable bags or freezer-safe containers. Do not defrost before baking but allow for an additional 3 minutes of cooking time.

Preheat the oven to 400°F. Line two baking sheets with parchment paper. Line one plate with parchment paper and a second plate with paper towels.

Arrange the bacon on one of the prepared baking sheets in a single layer. Grind or sprinkle black pepper liberally over the bacon. Bake for 10 minutes. Carefully pour off the fat and reserve. Continue to bake the bacon as needed until crisp, checking often. Pour 2 tablespoons of the reserved bacon fat onto the prepared plate with parchment paper and place into the freezer. Once crisp, remove the bacon from the oven and transfer the strips to the prepared plate with paper towels and set aside to cool completely.

Increase the oven temperature to 450°F. Sift 4 cups of the flour, the baking powder, baking soda, salt, and sugar over a large bowl. Finely chop the cooked bacon. Add the bacon, cheese, and chives to the flour mixture and toss gently, using your hand or a rubber spatula. Grate the frozen butter over the mixture using the large holes of a box grater. Remove the 2 tablespoons of bacon fat from the freezer and crumble it into the bowl. Using a rubber spatula, stir in the buttermilk until just combined, being careful not to overwork the dough. If too dry, add more buttermilk 1 tablespoon at a time as needed, until a soft sticky dough forms. Refrigerate the dough in the bowl for 10 minutes before continuing.

Transfer the dough to a floured surface. Fold the dough in half over itself, using your hands to gently flatten the layers together. If the dough sticks to your hands, sprinkle a little bit of flour over the dough. Repeat 5 to 6 times, rotating the dough 90 degrees each time, sprinkling more flour only as needed to prevent sticking to your hands without overworking the dough. Using a floured rolling pin, gently roll out the dough to about 1 inch thick.

Dip a 2½-inch (see notes) round cutter in flour and firmly press downward into the dough, then lift up without twisting, and place the biscuits on the prepared baking sheet. Continue cutting out the biscuits as closely together as possible, spacing them out evenly on the baking sheet, 1½ to 2 inches apart. Place the baking sheet with the biscuits into the freezer for 10 minutes (see notes). Remove from the freezer and bake for 12 to 15 minutes, or until golden brown (see notes).

Pull Me Out of the Pen Pork, Kansas Style

Yield: 10 to 12 servings; 4 cups barbecue sauce | GF

After Zeke rescues Dorothy from the pigpen when she falls in, he might need to be revived with a plate of this slow-cooked, seasoned pulled pork, topped with Auntie Em's Kansas City–style barbecue sauce. Thicker and sweeter than the classic version, it gets better the longer it sits in the icebox . . . er . . . refrigerator. Don't be afraid to mix it up a few days in advance. If you have any leftover pulled pork, use it to make sliders for lunch with Dinner on the Farm Rolls (page 15) or surprise everyone with Auntie Em's Prize-Winning Pulled Pork Cinnamon Rolls (page 16) for breakfast. Just don't tell the pigs.

FOR AUNTIE EM'S KANSAS CITY–STYLE BARBECUE SAUCE:

2 tablespoons salted butter

2 small yellow onions, finely chopped (about 2 cups)

6 medium garlic cloves, minced (about 2 tablespoons)

1½ teaspoons kosher salt, divided, plus more as needed

One 14-ounce can chopped or crushed fire-roasted tomatoes

1 cup ketchup

¾ cup packed brown sugar

½ cup apple cider vinegar

½ cup molasses

1 tablespoon smoked paprika

2 teaspoons freshly ground black pepper

1 teaspoon chile powder (optional)

½ teaspoon red pepper flakes (optional)

½ teaspoon ground mustard or 2 tablespoons yellow mustard

FOR THE PORK:

3 to 4 pounds boneless, well-marbled pork butt, trimmed of excess fat

About 1 tablespoon kosher salt

About ½ tablespoon freshly ground black pepper

About 2 cups of Auntie Em's Kansas City–style barbecue sauce, plus more to serve

1 to 4 cups of chicken stock, vegetable stock, or water, depending on the cooking method

TO MAKE THE BARBECUE SAUCE: Melt the butter in a small saucepan over medium heat. Add the onions, garlic, and 1 teaspoon of the salt. Sauté for 5 minutes, stirring. Reduce the heat to medium-low, cover, and cook for 7 to 10 minutes, or until soft, stirring occasionally.

Place the tomatoes, ketchup, brown sugar, vinegar, molasses, paprika, black pepper, chile powder, red pepper flakes, and mustard into a blender or food processor. Add the sautéed onion mix. Purée until smooth, adding ½ teaspoon of salt. Return to the saucepan. Bring to a boil over medium-high heat. Reduce heat to medium-low and simmer, uncovered, stirring often, for 50 to 60 minutes, until it has thickened and is coating the spoon. Taste for salt and pepper, adding more as needed. Allow the sauce to cool completely before using it to marinate the pork or refrigerate in an airtight container for up to a week.

TO MAKE THE PORK: In a large bowl, sprinkle the pork liberally with the salt and pepper. Allow it to sit for 20 minutes. Rub 1 to 1½ cups of the cooled barbecue sauce over the pork, massaging it into the meat. Cover the bowl with plastic wrap and refrigerate for at least two hours, or up to 2 days.

STOVETOP METHOD: Arrange the marinated pork in a large Dutch oven or heavy pot. Add the stock or water until it is about three-quarters of the way up the side of the pork. Brush the top of the meat liberally with more of the barbecue sauce. Cover the Dutch oven or pot and just bring to a boil over medium-high heat. Reduce the temperature to low and simmer for about 1 hour per pound, or until the meat begins to pull apart with a fork. Turn off the stove and let the meat rest for about 20 minutes. Place the meat into a large bowl and add in 1 cup of the cooking liquid. Using tongs or two forks, pull the pork apart.

OVEN METHOD: Preheat the oven to 300°F.

Arrange the marinated pork in a large Dutch oven or heavy casserole dish. Add the stock or water until it is about three-quarters of the way up the side of the pork. Brush the top of the meat liberally with more of the barbecue sauce. Cover with a heavy lid or wrap the pan tightly with foil. Place into the preheated oven. After 2 hours, reduce the heat to 250°F and continue cooking for a total of 1 hour per pound, or until the meat begins to pull apart with a fork. Remove from the oven and let the meat rest for about 20 minutes. Place the meat into a large bowl and add in 1 cup of the cooking liquid. Using tongs or two forks, pull the pork apart.

SLOW COOKER METHOD: Arrange the marinated pork in the slow cooker, cutting the pork into large pieces as needed to cover the bottom evenly. Add 1 cup of stock or water. Turn the slow cooker on to low and cook for 8 to 10 hours or on high for about 5 to 6 hours, or until the meat begins to pull apart with a fork. Allow to rest for 20 minutes. Using tongs or two forks, pull the pork apart into the cooking liquid, adding more barbecue sauce to taste.

Heat the remaining barbecue sauce in a small saucepan or a microwave. Add some to the pork to taste.

TO SERVE: Serve remaining sauce on the side or as a dip for Auntie Em's Prize-Winning Pulled Pork Cinnamon Rolls (page 16).

Old-Fashioned Lemonade

Yield: 8 servings | GF, V, V+

Slopping hogs in a dusty farmyard under a blazing sun. Harvesting corn on an August day. Singing wistfully on a piece of discarded farm machinery. A Kansas farm can be a thirsty place in the summer, which is why Auntie Em makes sure she always has a pitcher of fresh lemonade in the icebox.

1½ cups sugar

About 8 cups water, divided (see note)

8 to 10 lemons, juiced to make 2 cups

NOTES

To save room in your own icebox, make the lemonade base and sugar syrup combination ahead of time and chill, then mix with cold water just before serving.

Make the lemonade a little stronger knowing that the ice will dilute it slightly, especially if you do not have time or space to chill the lemonade before serving.

Place the sugar and 1½ cups water in a small saucepan and bring to a boil over medium-high heat, stirring until the sugar dissolves. Set aside to cool while you juice the lemons.

Combine the lemon juice with the sugar syrup. Store in an airtight container and refrigerate for up to 3 days.

Combine the lemonade base with 5 to 7 cups of cold water (see note). Chill for up to 24 hours in the refrigerator. Stir, then pour over ice into a pitcher or glasses to serve.

Grilled Sausages with Marvelous Campfire Spread

Yield: 8 servings | GF*

"One dog to another," Professor Marvel says when Toto steals his sausage. The magician might want to protect his meal by moving his feast indoors. There, he can create an edible campfire with a cheddar spread base and bacon "logs." Get out the toasting fork, Marvel!

FOR THE CHEDDAR BACON SPREAD:

6 slices of bacon or 3 slices thick-cut bacon

1 yellow onion, ¼-inch dice

2 cups freshly grated cheddar cheese (about 8 ounces; see note)

8 ounces cream cheese

¼ cup apple cider vinegar

½ to 1 tablespoon smoked paprika

FOR THE GRILLED SAUSAGES:

8 bratwurst or hot dogs

8 hot dog buns

NOTE

Shredded cheeses are treated with ingredients that prevent sticking. Freshly grated cheddar will give you a creamier spread. This recipe is easily made gluten-free by using gluten-free sausages.

TO MAKE THE CHEDDAR BACON SPREAD: In a large skillet over medium heat, cook the bacon until crisp. Drain on paper towels, leaving 2 tablespoons of the fat in the pan. In the same pan, sauté the onion, letting it caramelize over medium heat for about 20 minutes. Remove from the heat and add the cheddar cheese, cream cheese, and vinegar, stirring until the cheese melts. Return the pan to low heat and stir until the dip becomes creamy. Add ½ tablespoon smoked paprika, adding more to taste and reserving some to sprinkle on top before serving. Reserve the bacon pieces to decorate the spread as below.

TO MAKE THE GRILLED SAUSAGES: Preheat the oven to 400°F. Arrange in a single layer on a baking sheet. Bake for 10 to 15 minutes, until heated through and lightly browned. Place the sausages into the buns and return to the oven for 2 minutes.

TO SERVE: Place the warm spread into a serving bowl and place the bowl on a larger serving platter. Sprinkle the dip with paprika and pile the bacon "logs" into the middle. Arrange the sausages on the platter, around the "campfire," and serve immediately.

Professor Marvel's Crystal Ball Cookies

Yields 6 to 8 shaker cookies | V

When Professor Marvel gazes into his crystal ball, silk turban on his head and Dorothy watching anxiously at his side, he might wish he was seeing these special shaker cookies—inspired by that selfsame crystal ball. But you don't need a magical crystal ball for this recipe. Just isomalt, easily available at baking supply stores or online, and a little confidence in your kitchen skills. The extra assembly effort is worth it once you see your sparkly scenes encased in sugar cookie dough. Prop them up as table decorations for your guests to admire before they bite in. We predict that they won't last long at your gathering.

FOR THE DOUGH:

¾ cup salted butter, softened

4 ounces cream cheese, softened

¾ cup firmly packed light brown sugar

1 egg

1 teaspoon vanilla extract

3 cups all-purpose flour, plus more for dusting

About 6 ounces precooked isomalt pieces

FOR THE ICING:

4 cups powdered sugar, sifted

3 tablespoons meringue powder

6 tablespoons water

1 to 2 drops each blue and dark green food coloring

TO ASSEMBLE:

Edible markers

White or opal sanding sugar

Sprinkles, such as cows, chicks, fall leaves, and hearts

SPECIALTY TOOLS:

5-inch-tall snow globe cookie cutter

2½-inch circle cookie cutter

TO MAKE THE DOUGH: In a large bowl, beat together the butter, cream cheese, and sugar until light and fluffy. Add the egg and vanilla and beat again until well combined. Add the flour, 1 cup at a time, mixing on low and mixing by hand with the last cup.

Split the dough in half, form into disks, wrap in parchment paper, and chill for at least 1 hour. Toward the end of the hour, preheat the oven to 375°F. Line two baking sheets with silicone mats or parchment.

Place the isomalt crystals in a resealable bag and crush into smaller pieces, no larger than a pea. Place in a resealable container and set aside.

After chilling the dough, work with one half at a time on a lightly floured surface. Roll out each disk to ⅛ inch thick and cut out as many snow globes as you can with the cookie cutter (you will need three snow globes for each shaker cookie). Cut, from the center of two of the globes in each set, a circle. Remove the circle shape and use them for another purpose (such as clock faces for the Be Still, My Ticking Heart Cookies, page 158) or reroll with the scraps to make more globes. Place all the cookies on the prepared baking sheets. Chill for 10 minutes and then bake for 3 minutes.

After 3 minutes, remove the cookies from the oven and place the crushed isomalt in the center of one of each set, making sure it goes from edge to edge but does not stick up too much past the dough. Return to the oven and bake for another 7 to 9 minutes or until just starting to brown at the edges and the isomalt is completely melted. Remove from the oven and give the cookie sheet a few firm taps on a cutting board to release some of the bubbles from the isomalt. Allow to cool completely on the baking sheet, about 15 minutes.

Repeat with the second disk of dough.

TO MAKE THE ICING: In the bowl of a stand mixer fitted with the whisk attachment or a large mixing bowl if using a handheld mixer, combine the powdered sugar, meringue powder, and water. Whisk on low speed for 7 to 10 minutes, or until the icing holds stiff peaks. (If using a hand mixer, whisk on high speed for 10 to 12 minutes.)

✦✦✦ TIPS ✦✦✦

✦ Precooked isomalt is available online and in craft stores and specialty baking stores. It is very easy to work with and holds up well without absorbing moisture. You can substitute crushed hard candy for the shaker window but you will need to keep the cookies in an airtight container as soon as possible; they will last about 24 hours before the window begins to collapse.

✦ If possible, roll out the dough directly onto a silicone baking mat, use the cookie cutters as directed and remove the scraps of dough from the mat rather than moving the cut-out cookies. This will help the cookies keep their shape and match up well when assembled together.

✦ If you don't want to make shaker cookies, use the markers, sugar, and icing to create your scene on the snow globe directly on the snow globe shapes.

Divide the icing into three small bowls and use the food coloring to create blue icing in one bowl and dark green icing in another bowl. Keep the icing in the third bowl white for glue or other decorations/colors you may want to add. Transfer the icing to pastry bags fitted with writing tips.

TO DECORATE AND ASSEMBLE: Dip a small pastry brush in water to spread a bit of the light blue icing onto the center of the intact snow globe (this will be the background to your scene). Allow to dry completely, 20 to 30 minutes. Once dry, use the edible markers to draw the barn and/or house on the background. Take the center cookie, the one without the isomalt window, and pipe some icing "glue" all along the backside including on the base, leaving a ¼-inch border along the inside window edge. Gently press this spacer cookie onto the base cookie. Add your sprinkles to the center. Add your icing glue in the same way to the window cookie and gently press onto the assembled cookies, creating the completed stack of three. Do not move until completely dry, 30 minutes to 1 hour. Once dry you can use a bit of icing and your damp pastry brush to coat the outside of the cookies and sprinkle with sanding sugar to complete the illusion of a crystal ball. Decorate the base of the crystal ball as desired with the dark green icing. Allow to dry completely.

Store in an airtight container or seal each shaker cookie in a treat bag.

Farmhand Egg Sandwiches

Yield: 2 to 4 servings

If you've already made Pull Up to the Table Bacon Cheddar Biscuits (page 24) and defended them against Uncle Henry, then cutting them in half and layering crispy hash browns and jammy-yolk eggs in the middle makes quick and easy sandwiches for your own hungry farmhands. Like Hunk, you don't need a brain to see how good these are first thing in the morning.

4 bacon cheddar biscuits (page 24)

1 cup frozen hash brown potatoes

1 tablespoon olive or vegetable oil

½ teaspoon kosher or flake salt, divided

1 tablespoon plus 1 teaspoon salted butter

4 eggs

⅛ teaspoon ground pepper

NOTE

The biscuits need to rest in the freezer for 10 minutes before baking. If you make them in advance, freeze them on the tray for 1 hour and transfer them to a resealable bag. Do not defrost but bake them for up to 3 minutes longer.

Prepare the biscuits (see note). Preheat the oven to 450°F.

Spread the hash browns over half of a baking sheet. Drizzle with the oil and sprinkle with about ¼ teaspoon salt. Cut a piece of parchment to line the other side of the baking sheet, big enough to hold the number of biscuits you are baking. Place the four unbaked biscuits on the parchment side of the baking sheet. Bake for 12 to 15 minutes (see note), or until the biscuits are golden brown. Place the biscuits on a cooling rack and continue to cook the hash browns as needed, until crisp and golden brown, stirring and checking them every 5 minutes. Melt the butter and brush the tops of the hot biscuits, reserving the rest of the melted butter for frying the eggs.

Once the biscuits are out of the oven cooling, heat a large skillet or griddle over medium heat. Add the remaining butter, coating the pan evenly. If you have four ramekins, crack one egg into each ramekin before sliding them into the skillet. Alternatively, crack the eggs directly into the hot pan. Season with the remaining salt and the pepper. Allow the eggs to cook until the white is set and the edges become brown and crisp, about 3 minutes. Carefully flip the eggs and cook for another 1 to 1½ minutes for over-medium yolks, or up to 3 minutes if you prefer your eggs over hard.

Using a fork, halfway between the bottom and top, poke through to the center all around the edge of each biscuit. Pull gently to separate the top from the bottom. Place a fried egg on the bottom of the biscuit and top with the hash browns. Cover the hash browns with the top of the biscuit and serve.

Where Will It Land? Twister Cupcakes

Yield: 12 cupcakes | V

Whirling, swirling, screaming across the Kansas prairie, a tornado terrifies Dorothy as it sweeps her away, depositing her all the way over the rainbow in Munchkinland. These delightful twister cupcakes aren't scary, though—they're just cream cheese–swirled chocolate cake, topped with fluffy twists of frosting. The only danger in your kitchen might be the tornado of enthusiasm unleashed by your delighted eaters.

FOR THE CAKES:

8 ounces cream cheese, softened

1 teaspoon vanilla paste

¾ cup sugar, divided

2 eggs, divided

One 10-ounce package mini chocolate chips, divided

1½ cups all-purpose flour

1 teaspoon baking soda

½ teaspoon salt

5 tablespoons vegetable oil

1 cup coffee

FOR THE FROSTINGS:

1½ cups salted butter, softened, divided

3½ cups powdered sugar, divided

1 tablespoon milk

¼ cup black cocoa powder

¼ cup cocoa powder

1 tablespoon coffee

SPECIALTY TOOLS:

Two 12-ounce pastry bags

One 16-ounce pastry bag

TO MAKE THE CAKES: Preheat the oven to 350°F. Line a 12-cavity muffin pan with liners.

In a medium bowl, add the softened cream cheese, vanilla paste, ¼ cup of sugar, and 1 egg. Using a hand mixer fitted with a whisk attachment or whisk, beat the ingredients until well combined. Stir in ½ cup of the mini chocolate chips. Set aside.

In a microwave-safe bowl, melt an additional ½ cup of mini chocolate chips, stirring until smooth. Set aside.

In a small bowl, combine the flour, baking soda, and salt. Set aside.

In a medium bowl, whisk together the remaining ½ cup of sugar, the vegetable oil, and remaining egg. Stir in the melted chocolate until well combined. Alternate adding the flour and coffee until all the ingredients are combined and the batter is smooth. Stir in the remainder of the mini chocolate chips. Fill each muffin liner about one-third full with the chocolate cake batter. Add mounded tablespoons of cream cheese filling over the batter and use the remaining chocolate cake batter to cover. Bake for 20 to 25 minutes or until a cake tester comes out clean or with only a bit of cream cheese filling. Cool completely before frosting.

TO MAKE THE FROSTINGS: In the bowl of a stand mixer or large bowl with a hand mixer, add ¾ cup of butter and beat until light and fluffy. Slowly add 2 cups of powdered sugar, ½ cup at a time, beating after each addition. Add the milk and beat again for 30 seconds until the frosting is light and fluffy. Set aside.

Using a clean bowl and clean beaters, add the remaining ¾ cup of butter and beat until light and fluffy. Add the cocoa powders and mix until well combined. Slowly add the remaining 1½ cups of powdered sugar, ½ cup at time, and continue until all has been added. Add the coffee and beat again on high for 30 seconds until the frosting is light and fluffy.

Add the white frosting to one of the 12-ounce pastry bags and the chocolate frosting to the other. Put a large star tip into the 16-ounce pastry bag. Cut the ends off each of the 12-ounce bags, about 1½ inches up, creating a large opening. Place both bags, side by side, down into the 16-ounce bag. Squeeze the bag over a plate to test that both frostings are coming out, and adjust the bags as needed. Pipe a large swirl of frosting on each cupcake. Serve within 1 hour or refrigerate until serving. Allow to sit at room temperature for 30 minutes before serving.

Twister Shakes

Yield: 2 twister shakes | GF*, V

Twirling and whirling through Dorothy's Kansas farm, the unexpected and destructive twister Dorothy gets caught in picks up cows, Miss Gulch, and even a house. Our much more enjoyable version of a twister is swirly, too, but our cows are sprinkles and our whirls are whipped cream and chocolate sauce. Topped with a sprinkle-filled ice-cream cone and cookie crumbles, this shake will be delightful to slurp up as you make your first appearance over the rainbow.

½ cup heavy whipping cream

¾ cup crushed chocolate sandwich cookies (about 4 ounces), divided

2 chocolate ice-cream cones

1 tablespoon sprinkles, such as chocolate jimmies, cows, chicks, and fall leaves

1 cup milk of choice

2 cups vanilla ice cream

4 tablespoons chocolate sauce

SPECIALTY TOOLS:

Pastry bag fitted with a large round tip, such as an 808

2 tall glasses, chilled in the freezer

⊰— NOTE —⊱

This can easily be made gluten-free by using gluten-free sandwich cookies, cones, and sprinkles.

✦ ✦ ✦ TIP ✦ ✦ ✦

✦ You can add the chocolate swirl to the glasses ahead of time and leave them laying on their sides in the freezer until needed.

Add the cream to a large bowl and use a mixer fitted with whisk attachments to whip the cream until stiff peaks form. Fold in the crushed sandwich cookies, reserving 1 tablespoon for garnish.

Place the pastry bag in a tall glass and fill with the whipped cream. Refrigerate until needed.

Using a paring knife or small serrated knife, cut about 1 inch off the end of each ice-cream cone. Take the tip of the cone that you removed, invert it, and gently insert it into the now open end of the cone. Carefully holding the "plug" in with your finger, add half the sprinkles to each cone. Leave the cones resting on their sides on a plate until needed.

In a blender, add the milk and ice cream and blend until smooth. Use a squeeze bottle or paint brush to paint a swirl of chocolate onto the sides of each glass, and divide the remaining chocolate syrup between the two glasses, at the bottom. Split the milkshake between the two glasses. Use the pastry tip to press a few inches into the shake and squeeze out the cream, lifting toward the surface as you go. Finish with a swirl of cream on top of the shake. Repeat with the second shake and sprinkle each with the remaining cookie crumble. Top with the prepared ice-cream cone, narrow-end down. Serve immediately.

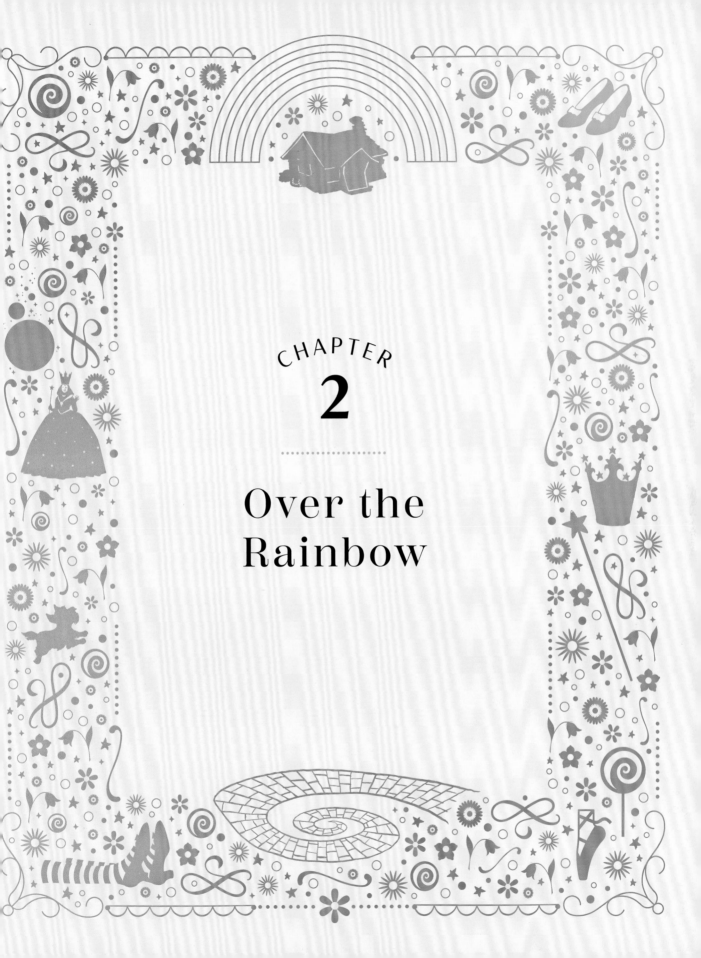

CHAPTER

2

Over the Rainbow

Over the Rainbow Crepe Cake

Yield: 6 to 12 servings | GF*, V

After the tornado, Dorothy finds herself in beautiful, colorful Munchkinland, surround by Glinda the Good Witch and all the munchkins. Thin, elegant crepes spread with fluffy vanilla cream cheese filling make for a gorgeous Hollywood moment when you cut into this unusual cake. Use food coloring to make different rainbow-colored crepes, then roll your creations around a strawberry sunset center framed by a perfect rainbow arch. No baking necessary—just wrap it tightly and refrigerate until it's firm. It's the perfect way to commemorate Dorothy's adventure over the rainbow.

FOR THE CREPES:

8 tablespoons unsalted butter, divided

1½ cups whole milk

½ cup cold heavy cream

1¼ cups all-purpose flour or gluten-free 1-to-1 flour

½ teaspoon kosher salt

4 tablespoons sugar

5 large eggs, room temperature

Food coloring gel for each color of the rainbow (see note)

1 pint fresh strawberries

FOR THE CREAM CHEESE FILLING:

1 cup heavy cream

8 ounces cream cheese, softened to room temperature

1 cup powdered sugar

½ tablespoon vanilla extract

Notes

Buying individual colors of food coloring gel will give you the most control, but you can also use red, yellow, and blue and combine accordingly. Start with one drop at a time until you achieve the color you are looking for.

This recipe is gluten-free if using gluten-free 1-to-1 flour.

TO MAKE THE CREPES: In a microwave-safe ramekin or small bowl, heat 6 tablespoons butter in a microwave, heating for 15 seconds at a time and stirring, until melted. In a blender, combine the milk, heavy cream, flour, salt, sugar, eggs, and the melted butter. Blend until the mixture is well blended and smooth. Let the batter sit in the blender at room temperature for 15 minutes while you make and then refrigerate the filling.

TO MAKE THE CREAM CHEESE FILLING: Add the heavy cream to a large mixing bowl or the bowl of a stand mixer. Use a hand mixer or the whisk attachment to beat the cream on high speed until medium-stiff peaks form, 5 to 7 minutes. Transfer the whipped cream into another bowl. Add the cream cheese to the now emptied bowl. Sift the powdered sugar over the cream cheese. Switching to a paddle attachment, or using your hand mixer, add the vanilla and beat until thick and smooth. Using a rubber spatula, fold the whipped cream into the cream cheese mixture, ½ cup at a time. Refrigerate for 30 to 60 minutes, or overnight for a more spreadable consistency.

After making the filling, preheat the oven to 400°F. Line a large baking sheet with parchment paper for cooling your cooked crepes. Put an ungreased quarter sheet pan into the oven to heat it up. Using a 10- to 16-ounce jar with a tight-fitting lid, pour ½ cup of the crepe batter into the jar. Add one drop of yellow food coloring gel. Cover the jar with the lid and shake vigorously. Adjust color by adding another drop of color at a time and shaking between each addition.

Remove the hot pan from the oven and lightly grease with some of the remaining butter, remembering that the pan is hot.

HINT: Rubbing the pan with one end of a stick of butter is the easiest and fastest way to grease a hot pan.

Using an oven mitt, lift one side of the hot pan and pour the batter along the top edge of the pan. Lift the pan and swirl the batter to evenly cover the pan. Place in the preheated oven for 5 minutes. Remove and place the pan upside down on a cooling rack to cool for 5 minutes. If you have a second quarter sheet pan, place it in the oven now to heat.

If you are working with one pan, gently remove the crepe from the sheet pan. If it sticks, very gently coax it from underneath with a bench scraper, a metal spatula, or a butter knife. It is perfectly fine if there are slight tears in the middle layers. Place the crepe on the parchment-lined baking sheet to cool completely. Rinse off any stuck pieces of crepe and place the pan in the oven for 5 minutes to get hot.

Continue to make 2 orange, 2 red, 1 purple, 1 blue, and 1 green crepe, following the directions for the yellow, making sure the pan is hot and greased again each time before adding the batter. Rinse the jar as needed to start a new color (yellow into orange does not need rinsing, etc.).

Once all the crepes are completely cool, place a 3-foot piece of parchment paper down on a work surface. Take the filling from the refrigerator. Wipe the strawberries well with a paper towel. If you wash the strawberries, make sure they are very dry before continuing.

Fold the purple crepe in half so the short ends meet. Place the folded end in the center of the parchment, on the edge closest to you. Using an offset or rubber spatula, spread the entire surface of the purple crepe with about ½ inch of filling. Lay out the blue crepe lengthwise, tucking one shorter edge under the edge on the far side of the purple crepe. Spread a thin, even layer of filling over the blue crepe. Slice the ends off each strawberry. One inch from the folded purple edge, make one line of strawberries, making sure they are touching, from one end to the other. Tightly roll the purple crepe over the strawberries and continue rolling until you have run out of blue crepe. Carefully lift the roll and bring it back to your end of the parchment paper. Place the green crepe down on the parchment in front of the roll. Spread another thin, even layer of filling over the entire surface. Place the roll on top of the green crepe, making sure to match the edges. Roll until you reach the end of the green crepe. Continue with the yellow crepe, 1½ orange crepes (by cutting the second orange crepe in half) and finish with the 2 red crepes. Using a paper towel, wipe any excess filling from the parchment paper. Roll the crepe roll tightly with the parchment paper and twist the ends. Fold the ends down and place in the refrigerator for at least 4 hours or overnight.

To serve, cut about ½ inch off each end. Cut the roll into slices, and then slice in half through the center to create your rainbows. Arrange them standing up. If you are creating any boards, be sure to include a rainbow!

Savory Sweet Potato Tartlets*

Yield: 9 servings | V, V+*

The flowers of Munchkinland come to life in this tartlet recipe, which may seem complicated but is actually quite easy. Droplets of honey help "glue" together potato-slice petals before baking upside down. Flip your savory little pastries at the end and enjoy the sesame-sprinkled flower effect.

Three 1½-inch- to 2-inch-diameter sweet potatoes, including purple and yellow flesh varieties if available

1 tablespoon olive oil

1 teaspoon salt, divided

½ teaspoon paprika

1 tablespoon honey

1 tablespoon black or white sesame seeds

5 ounces goat cheese or creamy plant-based cheese

1 sheet frozen puff pastry, thawed

Note

This recipe is easily made vegan by using maple syrup in place of honey and a plant-based creamy cheese.

Preheat the oven to 400°F. Line a baking sheet with parchment paper.

Using a mandoline or a sharp knife, thinly slice the sweet potatoes. Place in a bowl with the olive oil, ½ teaspoon of salt, and the paprika. Toss until the slices are well coated.

Evenly space out nine dots of honey, about 4 inches apart on the prepared baking sheet. Using a small spoon, sprinkle the sesame seeds over the honey to just cover. Push any stragglers up against the honey. Divide the slices of sweet potatoes into nine equal stacks, keeping the colors the same or as similar as possible. Place the lower edge of one of the sweet potato circles on the top half of a honey dot. Overlap the sweet potatoes in a circular pattern, leaving about ⅛ inch from one edge to the next, around and completely covering the honey dot, to create a flower shape. Continue with the rest of the flowers. Top the flowers with about 1 tablespoon of goat cheese and the remaining ½ teaspoon salt.

Place the thawed puff pastry on a cutting board or work surface and cut into nine squares. Place one square of puff pastry over each goat cheese–topped flower and press gently to spread out the goat cheese slightly.

Bake for about 18 minutes or until golden brown. Remove from the oven and let rest for 15 minutes. Using a metal spatula, carefully slide under each flower and invert onto a cooling rack, pastry-side down. Cool for 10 minutes before serving.

Rainbow Crudités and Hummus

Yield: 12 servings; 3 cups hummus base; 2 cups each yellow and red hummus;
1 to 2 cups purple hummus (makes 1 cup if using sweet potato powder) | GF, V, V+

Rainbow flavors can be savory as well as sweet, as in this multicolored vegetable and hummus board inspired by the beautiful array of colors in Munchkinland. Creamy red, yellow, and purple hummus dips accompany crisp crudités and chips. You only need to make one hummus base before mixing in peppers, spices, and veggies to create unique colors and flavors.

FOR THE HUMMUS BASE:

Two 15-ounce cans chickpeas, drained, reserving the liquid

2 cloves garlic, roughly chopped or smashed

4 tablespoons olive oil

½ cup tahini paste

½ lemon, juiced

½ teaspoon salt, plus more as needed

FOR THE YELLOW HUMMUS:

2 yellow peppers, roasted (see directions below)

1 teaspoon turmeric or curry powder, divided

FOR THE RED HUMMUS:

2 red peppers, roasted (see directions below)

¾ teaspoon smoked paprika, plus more as needed

¼ teaspoon cumin, plus more as needed

FOR THE PURPLE HUMMUS:

1 purple sweet potato or 2 large purple carrots, peeled and cut into 1-inch chunks (see note)

1 tablespoon olive oil

6 to 8 cloves black garlic, roughly chopped

TO MAKE THE HUMMUS BASE: Add the chickpeas and chopped garlic to a blender or the bowl of a food processor. Measure the olive oil into a ½-cup measuring cup and add to the chickpeas. Measure the tahini using the same ½-cup measuring cup and watch it slide easily into the chickpea mixture. Add the lemon juice to the blender or food processor and process for about 2 minutes, stopping to scrape the sides. Add salt to taste and process for another minute. This is the base that will take on additional flavors and will be further seasoned as you go along. If you are using this hummus as is, season it to taste accordingly.

Transfer the hummus to a quart-size bowl. Use as prepared or as a base for the following color options.

TO ROAST THE RED OR YELLOW PEPPERS: Preheat the oven to 400°F. Place the peppers on a baking sheet and roast for about 40 minutes, turning them with tongs halfway through, until they have collapsed and the skins look charred.

Remove the baking sheet from the oven and place the peppers on a plate. Cover them immediately with an upside-down bowl and let rest for 15 minutes. This allows the peppers to steam, making it easier to remove the skins. Cut the peppers in half, peel off any skin that comes off easily, and scrape out the seeds, rinsing under water to help remove any stubborn bits. Pat dry with paper towels.

TO MAKE THE YELLOW HUMMUS: Add the roasted yellow peppers and turmeric or curry to the bowl of a food processor or blender (see note) and pulse. Add 1 cup of the hummus base and blend until smooth. Taste for salt and seasoning, adding more as needed. Transfer into a serving bowl and refrigerate until ready to serve, up to 3 days. Note: If you have just made the hummus base and transferred it into another bowl, there is no need to clean it before making the first flavored hummus. In between colors, just give the container a good rinse and shake and move on to the next color.

FOR THE RAINBOW CRUDITÉS:

Look for about 4 to 5 pounds total divided among the different-color vegetables you are using. Your choices can be made based on your preferences or what is available, trying to cover as many colors of the rainbow as possible, adding in any options not listed that catch your eye.

Red: red peppers, cherry tomatoes, radishes, beets,

Orange: orange peppers, carrots, orange cauliflowers, orange cherry tomatoes

Yellow: yellow peppers, yellow summer squash, yellow cherry tomatoes, yellow beets

Green: green beans, snap peas, cucumber, celery, broccoli, zucchini

Blue: blue corn chips, blue potato chips

Purple: purple cauliflower, purple carrots, radicchio, purple endive

TO MAKE THE RED HUMMUS: Add the roasted red pepper, smoked paprika, and cumin to the bowl of a food processor or blender and pulse. Add in 1 cup of the hummus base and process until smooth. Taste for salt and seasonings, adding more as needed. Transfer into a serving bowl and refrigerate until ready to serve, up to 3 days.

TO MAKE THE PURPLE HUMMUS: Preheat the oven to 400°F. Place the purple sweet potatoes or purple carrots on one side of a sheet of aluminum foil about 1½ feet long, leaving room on all sides. Toss with olive oil and a pinch of salt and fold the aluminum, sealing it tightly by crimping the edges. Place on a baking sheet (this can be the same baking sheet used to roast the peppers). Bake for 30 to 40 minutes, or until tender. Remove from the oven and allow to cool for 15 minutes.

Add the black garlic and 1 cup of the hummus base to the bowl of a food processor or blender and process for 1 minute to combine. Add the cooked purple sweet potato or purple carrots and process another 1 to 2 minutes, adding water or chickpea liquid and salt as needed. Transfer into a serving bowl and refrigerate until ready to serve, up to 3 days.

TO MAKE THE RAINBOW CRUDITÉS:

Select a variety of the vegetables listed, trying to cover as many colors of the rainbow as possible.

Place the bowls of hummus on your platter. Cut the vegetables and arrange the platter by color in sequence of a rainbow, from red to purple, around the bowls and leaving room for chips if using. Cover and refrigerate without adding the chips for up to 2 hours. Add the chips, if using, just before serving.

Notes

Purple vegetables can be hard to find. A good alternative is adding 3 to 4 teaspoons, or more, of purple sweet potato powder, and adding water or chickpea liquid to achieve a creamy consistency. We will be using purple sweet potato powder again to make Festive Munchkin Goodwitches (page 61).

Save the leftover chickpea liquid for other recipes, like the Fuzzy Mitten (page 157). Just pour it into a jar and refrigerate.

Savory Pinwheel Lollipops

Yield: About 24 pinwheels

Dorothy is welcomed to Munchkinland by all sorts of Munchkins, including the scowly, dancing Lollipop Guild. Like the giant lollipop the guild presents to Dorothy, these savory pinwheels are swirly and delicious—and a great way to use up leftover Marvelous Campfire Spread (page 31). After rolling, slicing, and skewering, we like to arrange these lollies in a narrow glass or vase to show off their spiral insides.

2 cups (1 recipe) Marvelous Campfire Spread (page 31), room temperature, or pub cheese

4 large green sandwich wraps

12 ounces sliced deli style turkey

SPECIALTY TOOLS:
About 24 skewers

Follow the directions for the Marvelous Campfire Spread, mixing the bacon into the cheddar mixture. Place one sandwich wrap on a work surface. Spread a thin layer, up to one-quarter of the spread, over the entire wrap. Layer up to 3 ounces turkey over two-thirds of the wrap, leaving one-third of the spread to act as the glue. Begin tightly rolling the turkey side toward the spread side, adjusting the turkey slices as needed if they shift. Roll tightly in plastic wrap, twisting the sides to seal. Repeat with the remaining wraps. Place seam-side down into the refrigerator and chill overnight or for up to 2 days, keeping them safe from anything that could fall down on them. Remove from the plastic, cut off about 1 inch at each end of the rolls (delicious for snacking), and cut into ¾-inch slices. Skewer each pinwheel through the seam-side and display the savory lollipops in a narrow glass or vase.

Glittery Glinda Cake

Yield: 32 to 36 servings | V

Glinda the Good Witch appears in the burst of a magical bubble, then glitters before Dorothy in a sea of frothy pink and sparkly silver. Our Glittery Glinda Cake captures some of her ethereal sweetness with a tower of raspberry sponge cakes, encrusted with edible glitter, stars, and, for a finishing flourish, clear pink bubbles made with isomalt. You can just picture Dorothy enjoying a slice of this confection as she's serenaded by the Munchkins and welcomed by Glinda herself.

FOR THE CAKES:

2½ cups milk

½ teaspoon rose water

1 tablespoon lemon juice

2 tablespoons freeze-dried raspberry powder (see note)

3 whole eggs

3 egg whites

4½ cups flour

½ cup cornstarch

2 cups sugar

2½ tablespoons baking powder

1 teaspoon salt

1½ cups unsalted butter

FOR THE FROSTING:

1 cup meringue powder

1½ cups water

2⅔ cups sugar

5 cups (2½ pounds) unsalted butter, softened

2 tablespoons freeze-dried raspberry powder

TO MAKE THE CAKES: Line the bottom of each cake pan with rounds of parchment paper and preheat the oven to 350°F.

In a large bowl, add the milk, rose water, lemon juice, and raspberry powder, and whisk to combine. Add the eggs and egg whites one at a time, whisking after each addition. Set aside.

In the bowl of a stand mixer fitted with a paddle attachment or a large mixing bowl if using a hand mixer, add the flour, cornstarch, sugar, baking powder, and salt. Stir to combine. Add the butter and stir on low until the mixture is a coarse crumb with most of the butter broken up to pea-size pieces.

Add all but ½ cup of the milk mixture to the flour mixture and beat on medium speed for about 2 minutes. Scrape down the sides of the bowl, add the remaining milk mixture, and beat again for about 1 minute more. Fill each 8-inch cake pan with 4 cups of batter and each 6-inch cake pan with 1½ cups of batter. Bake for 25 to 30 minutes, rotating the cakes halfway through. If your oven is small, bake the big cakes first and the smaller ones second. The cakes are done when a cake tester comes out clean. The smaller cakes may cook a bit faster, so check them after 20 minutes.

Allow to cool on wire racks for 15 minutes before removing from the cake pans. Allow to cool completely on wire racks before frosting and decorating.

TO MAKE THE FROSTING: Combine the meringue powder, water, and sugar in a medium saucepan over medium-high heat. Whisk continuously for 3 to 4 minutes until the mixture is warm and foamy and has no graininess when you run it through your fingers.

Pour the meringue mixture into the bowl of a stand mixer fitted with a whisk attachment or a large mixing bowl if using a handheld mixer, and beat on high until the sides of the bowl are cool to the touch. This may take up to 5 minutes.

While the meringue is whipping, cut the butter into tablespoon-size pieces and have standing by. Once the meringue is cool, reduce the speed to medium-high and begin adding the butter, one piece at a time. Wait about 15 to 20

TO ASSEMBLE:

7 ounces clear, cooked isomalt pieces

7 ounces pink, cooked isomalt pieces (see note)

Glitter sugar, in pinks, silver, and gold (optional)

Gold and silver foil stars (optional)

1 pound fresh raspberries, rinsed, drained, and dried

Powdered sugar, for dusting

SPECIALTY TOOLS:

Two 8-inch cake pans

Two 6-inch cake pans

Cake board or cake plate

4-inch cardboard cake round (see note)

Silicone circle molds (optional)

seconds for each piece of butter to be incorporated. Continue adding pieces until all the butter has been incorporated. In the middle of this process, the mixture may look soupy but should come together once all the butter has been added. Add the raspberry powder and mix on high for about 30 seconds. Scrape down the sides of the bowl and whisk again to make sure all the powder is incorporated.

TO MAKE THE ISOMALT BUBBLES: Line a baking sheet with parchment paper and place it on a heatproof surface. Melt a few pieces of the isomalt at a time in a microwave-safe bowl in 30-second bursts. Combine the clear and pink pieces to create different shades of pink. Pour the isomalt onto the parchment paper, creating different-size circles, creating 1 to 3 at a time. Sprinkle with sugar and stars as desired. Continue to melt the isomalt until you have created 10 to 12 bubbles, or the desired amount. You may want to pour some of the circles over lollipop sticks to create height for the top of the cake. Perfect circles can be made by pouring the isomalt into silicone molds or greasing round cookie cutters.

TO ASSEMBLE THE CAKE: Cut each cake in half horizontally, forming 4 layers from each size. Place an 8-inch layer on a cake board or cake plate. Use 1 cup of frosting to fill this layer. Press 6 ounces of raspberries into the frosting, starting by creating a ring close to the edge and filling in the center. Dust the berries with a thin layer of powdered sugar. Place a second 8-inch cake layer on top and gently press to level the layer. Use an additional 1 cup of frosting to fill this layer and top with a third 8-inch cake layer. Add another 1 cup of frosting and another 6 ounces of raspberries. Continue to gently level as you add layers. Top with the remaining 8-inch layer. Use another 1 cup of frosting to fill the gaps between the layers and crumb coat the entire cake by adding a thin layer of frosting. Then chill for 20 minutes. After 20 minutes, finish frosting the top and exterior of the cake.

Building on the 4-inch cake round, repeat this process with the 6-inch cake layers, using ½ cup of frosting to fill each layer and split the remaining raspberries between the first and third layers.

When ready to display and serve (see below), stack the 6-inch cake onto the 8-inch cake, slightly off center. Decorate with the isomalt circles, gently pressing them to the side, setting them on the ledge between the tiers and adding them to the top.

NOTE: Cake strips (see glossary) can help bake very even cakes, usually without the domed tops. If you don't use cake strips, you may end up with three cake layers of each size instead of four. This is totally fine—you will just have a bit of extra frosting and berries.

The 4-inch cake round will add structure to the tiered cake and make it easier for you to move the 6-inch cake around until final assembly. If the cake is going to be on display for longer than 1 hour, you may want to consider cake dowels for extra support. Cake dowels can be made of paper, like a lollipop stick, wood, or even plastic straws. They would be inserted into the center of the

8-inch tier (three or four should work) and cut to sit just below the buttercream on the top layer. This helps keep the 6-inch tier from tilting or sinking into the tier below.

SERVING AND STORING: The cake layers can be made up to 3 days in advance, wrapped in plastic or stored in an airtight container in the refrigerator.

The frosting can be stored in an airtight container in the refrigerator for up to 1 week but must be brought back to room temperature before stirring and using.

The isomalt circles can be made up to 3 days ahead if stored in an airtight container between layers of parchment.

The assembled tiers can be stored, separately, without the decoration, in the refrigerator for up to 24 hours. If the display temperature is moderate the cake can be set up with its decor for up to 3 hours, if it has been chilled prior to setup.

Good Witch Pink Lemonade

Yield: 8 servings | GF, V, V+

Glinda the Good Witch floats into Munchkinland inside a beautiful pink bubble. Then she appears in front of Dorothy in all her sparkly splendor, captivating Dorothy with both her kindness and beauty. We captured some of Glinda's pink sweetness with this watermelon lemonade. Use the base from the Old-Fashioned Lemonade (page 29) and just add puréed watermelon before chilling. Make a few more Glinda bubbles with flower ice cubes—use edible flowers, distilled water, and sphere ice molds.

4 cups cubed seedless watermelon (about one 4-pound watermelon)

2 cups Old-Fashioned Lemonade base (page 29; see note)

3 to 4 cups cold water

Note

Old-Fashioned Lemonade Base is the simple syrup and lemon juice mix, before adding water to taste.

Add the watermelon to a blender or food processor and pulse until well puréed. Pour through a fine-mesh strainer into a bowl. Pour the strained watermelon into a 1-gallon pitcher or jar. Add the Old-Fashioned Lemonade Base and stir. Chill in the refrigerator for at least 2 hours.

When ready to serve, remove from the refrigerator and stir. Add the cold water to taste and pour over ice either into a pitcher or directly into glasses. Serve immediately.

Ruby-Red Punch

Yield: 8 servings | GF, V, V+

This punch won't bring you home from a magical land, but it will look beautiful when poured into pretty glasses with a red-rose sugar rim. Red grapefruit and lemon juice give this beverage a fresh citrus zing, and the Cordial Munchkin Sweetness (page 69) hibiscus syrup swirls in a magnificent ruby color. It may not be as powerful as Dorothy's slippers—but what it lacks in power, it makes up for in its refreshing flavors and beautiful vibrant color.

FOR THE ROSE-SUGAR RIM:

2 tablespoons sugar or red sanding sugar

2 tablespoons dried red rose petals

FOR THE PUNCH:

4 ruby-red grapefruits, juiced (about 2 cups)

½ cup lemon juice (about 2 lemons)

1 cup Cordial Munchkin Sweetness hibiscus syrup, divided (page 69)

6 cups still or sparkling water

TO MAKE THE ROSE-SUGAR RIM: Grind the sugar and rose petals together in a spice grinder, mortar and pestle, or blender. Place on a plate and set aside until needed.

TO MAKE THE PUNCH: Combine the grapefruit juice with the lemon juice into a 1-quart jar or measuring cup, or a pitcher. Add the hibiscus syrup to taste. Chill in the refrigerator for 2 to 24 hours.

When ready to serve, dip the glasses into the punch and then into the rose sugar mixture. Fill the prepared glasses, or a pitcher, with ice and pour in the grapefruit mixture, leaving room for still or sparkling water to taste.

Ding-Dong Graham Cracker House

Yield: 1 house | V

"Ding-dong, the witch is dead!" the joyful Munchkins sing, and there she is, the Wicked Witch of the East—iconic ruby slippers sticking out from under the tornado-tossed house. Take a slow afternoon and re-create this scene with a graham-cracker-and-royal-icing house and gumdrop ruby slippers. And don't worry if your house winds up a little wonky—it has been through a twister, after all.

½ recipe royal icing, from the Professor Marvel's Crystal Ball Cookies (page 32)

11 full graham crackers, plus a few more in case of breakage

½ cup semisweet chocolate chips

2 black licorice twists

4 small red gumdrops

Food coloring, such as green, pink, and red (optional)

4 honey-wheat twisted pretzel sticks

Edible moss

1 egg

1 teaspoon maple syrup

1 tablespoon sugar

3 tablespoons all-purpose flour

1½ teaspoons baking powder

1 to 3 drops green food coloring

¼ cup yellow jimmies

SPECIALTY TOOLS:
Pastry bag fitted with a writing tip

Place about 1 cup of white royal icing in a pastry bag fitted with a writing tip, stand up in a tall glass, and have standing by. Have the desired serving platter or board that you wish to build on standing by.

Use a small serrated knife to create the roof peaks with a full sheet of graham cracker. Looking at the long side of a full graham cracker, cut off the top corners, starting at the center line and finishing at the lower corner. Repeat, creating two roof peaks. Save any breakage or scraps to create rubble, if desired.

Lay out the house pieces: the two roof peaks you just created and four full graham crackers. Pipe the windows as desired on the full graham cracker pieces (the front, back, or sides of the house). Pipe thin lines of icing, one at a time, going around the windows, and brush them with a barely damp pastry brush. Allow to dry for at least 30 minutes and add more details, such as flowers or vines. Allow to dry completely. Use more icing to "glue" the long side of each roof peak to the long side of one of the full graham crackers, creating the ends of the house.

Once everything is dry, you can begin to build the house. As you build the house, consider where you want the front to be (your favorite end) and leave enough room for the edible moss and yellow brick road, if using. Place an end piece and a side piece (another decorated full graham cracker) together perpendicular to each other, using icing as a glue. You can gently hold these until set or brace them against something like small canned goods. Repeat with the other end and side. Once those are set, about 15 to 30 minutes, glue the two halves of the house together to create a full square. Allow to dry for at least 30 minutes.

To place the roof, take one full graham cracker and line it up with the point of the peak on one side, and use icing to glue. Place another full graham cracker below the first one, allowing the extra to hang off the house. This will create the porch covering. On the other side, place the two remaining full graham crackers and glue them at jaunty angles, leaving a gap if necessary. The house has been through a twister, after all!

While the house is drying, make the edible moss: In a microwave-safe bowl, add the egg, maple syrup, and sugar and whisk until well combined. Add the flour and baking powder and whisk again. Add the food coloring and whisk until uniform in color. Microwave for 1½ to 2 minutes, until the cake is firm but spongy. Allow to cool and, using your hands or a spatula, remove from the bowl. Break apart as desired to create the yellow brick road and surrounding environment. Make sure to tilt one side of the house up with some of the moss. Pipe the licorice twists with white icing to make striped stockings. Mold each gumdrop into a ruby slipper and use icing to attach it to a candy stick. Place the slippers sticking out from under the corner of the house.

Melt the chocolate chips in a microwave-safe bowl, using 30-second bursts, and stir until smooth. Use a clean pastry or craft brush to brush the "roof tiles" onto the roof with the melted chocolate, starting with the bottom row and working up. Split another full graham cracker in half lengthwise and use the chocolate to brush the "boards" onto the porch. Place this graham cracker flat next to the house but still touching it to create the porch. Add the honey-wheat pretzel sticks to the corner of the porch, gluing in place with icing. Place the porch under the roof overhang.

Festive Munchkin Goodwitches

Yield: 64 sandwiches | V*

Colorful homemade rolls! Curried apricot mayonnaise! Brie with strawberry red wine jam! Call them sliders, call them tea sandwiches, but no matter what, call them festive. Like the Munchkins twirling around their new friend Dorothy, these Goodwitches make a beautiful, colorful display when spread out on your table decorated with your best linens.

FOR THE GOODWITCH ROLLS (SEE NOTE):

2 cups whole milk, divided

5 tablespoons water

5 to 6 cups all-purpose flour, plus more as needed, divided

⅓ cup granulated sugar

2 teaspoons kosher salt or 1 teaspoon fine salt

1½ tablespoons instant yeast (2 standard packets)

⅔ cup unsalted butter, room temperature, divided

2 large eggs, room temperature

To make blue: 2 teaspoons butterfly flower powder

To make yellow: 2 teaspoons turmeric

To make purple: 2 teaspoons purple sweet potato flower

To make green: 1½ teaspoons turmeric mixed with ½ teaspoon butterfly powder

Oil, for greasing

Notes

Divide the dough into 4 disks to create the 4 colors.

This recipe is easily made vegetarian by making only the Brie and the cucumber options.

TO MAKE THE GOODWITCH ROLLS: Measure the milk in a microwave-safe 1-quart measuring cup or medium-size bowl. Spoon 5 tablespoons of the measured milk and the water into a small saucepan. Add 4 teaspoons of the flour. Whisk constantly over medium heat until the mixture thickens, making distinct lines in the paste. Take the slurry off the heat and set it aside to cool to room temperature.

In a large bowl, combine 4 cups of the flour, the sugar, salt, and yeast. Whisk until combined (no need to clean the whisk between procedures). Heat the remaining milk until warm, about 110°F. Whisk half of the butter (6 tablespoons) and the eggs into the cooled flour paste. Whisk in the warm milk until well combined.

Using the rubber spatula to stir, slowly add the milk mixture into the flour-sugar mixture. Fold until the flour has been incorporated. Cover with plastic wrap or a tea towel and allow to sit at room temperature for 20 minutes.

Separate the still gooey dough into 4 bowls. Large plates will work if you are short on bowls. Starting with one section, sprinkle one of the four colors over the dough and knead it in with a rubber spatula. Add in ¼ cup of flour. Turn the dough out onto a floured surface and knead with your hands, sprinkling in more flour as needed until it is smooth and still slightly sticky. Place the dough into an oiled medium bowl or 1-gallon resealable bag. Rinse your hands and wipe any remaining color from the work surface before moving on to the next color. Repeat with the three remaining colors. Cover with plastic wrap or seal the resealable bag and refrigerate the dough for up to 24 hours (see note) or move on to the next rise.

Place in a warm, draft-free area and let rise until doubled. The time this takes varies greatly, depending on the temperature of your kitchen, taking anywhere from 45 to 90 minutes. It helps to set a timer for 15-minute intervals so you can check on how the dough is rising.

Using some of the reserved butter, grease a rimmed 9-by-13-inch baking dish or two 8-inch square or round cake pans. Divide each color into 16 pieces and shape into smooth balls. Place 32 balls in each pan, separating the colors with a strip of parchment paper.

FOR THE CURRIED APRICOT MAYONNAISE:

2 shallots, finely minced

1 tablespoon olive oil, plus more for greasing

½ cup apricot jam

1 tablespoon curry powder

2 tablespoons yellow or honey mustard

½ cup mayonnaise

Salt

Freshly ground black pepper

FOR THE SAVORY BLUEBERRY JAM:

½ cup blueberry jam

1 tablespoon lemon juice

⅛ teaspoon allspice

½ teaspoon cumin

Freshly ground black pepper

FOR THE STRAWBERRY RED WINE JAM:

2 tablespoons dry red wine, like pinot noir

2 tablespoons balsamic vinegar

½ cup strawberry jam

FOR THE TURKEY GOODWITCHES:

16 Goodwitch Rolls, sliced in half horizontally (see note)

Savory Blueberry Jam

Butter or mayonnaise, for the rolls (optional)

½ pound deli turkey, very thinly sliced (see note)

4 slices Swiss cheese, cut into 16 squares

2 green onion stalks, cut thinly on a diagonal

TO MAKE THE CURRIED APRICOT MAYONNAISE: In a small saucepan over medium heat, sauté the shallots in the olive oil until soft but not yet brown, about 5 minutes. Add the apricot jam and the curry. Cook for another 5 minutes. Remove from the heat and allow to cool. Once the mixture and the saucepan are completely cooled, add the mustard and mayonnaise, stirring until thoroughly mixed. Add salt and pepper to taste. Transfer to a serving bowl or airtight container and refrigerate for at least 2 hours or up to 5 days.

TO MAKE THE SAVORY BLUEBERRY JAM: In a small saucepan over medium-low heat, combine the jam, lemon juice, allspice, and cumin. Bring the mixture to a simmer and cook for 5 minutes, adding pepper to taste. Transfer into a bowl or jar and allow to cool. Keeps for up to 1 week.

TO MAKE THE STRAWBERRY RED WINE JAM: In a small saucepan, simmer the wine and vinegar together over medium-high heat until it has reduced by half. Stir in the jam and remove from the heat. Smash down any larger pieces of strawberry with a fork or the back of a spoon. Transfer into a bowl or jar and allow to cool. Keeps for up to 1 week.

TO MAKE THE TURKEY GOODWITCHES: Spread the savory blueberry jam on the top half of 16 sliced rolls and spread the bottom half with butter or mayonnaise, if using. Fold 16 pieces of turkey in half lengthwise (see note). Fold it again as needed to fit the roll, giving the turkey height. Lay the folded turkey stack on the bottom half of the roll and top with a square of cheese. Cover the cheese with 2 or 3 slices of green onion, top with the prepared top half of the roll, and skewer with a toothpick.

Note

The rolls will brown slightly as they bake. Optionally, slice the tops off each roll for more color. Divide your meat slices and cheese into 16 pieces before assembling. Very thinly sliced meats allow you to fold each slice lengthwise and then fold it again (ribbon style) to achieve height. If you are unable to fold the slices, cut them into squares slightly larger than the cut surface of the rolls and stack about 5 squares to build the sandwiches.

FOR THE ROAST BEEF GOODWITCHES:

16 Goodwitch Rolls, sliced in half horizontally (see note)

Curried Apricot Mayonnaise

½ pound roast beef, very thinly sliced (see note)

4 slices cheddar, cut into 16 squares

½ cup arugula

FOR THE BRIE GOODWITCHES:

16 Goodwitch Rolls, sliced in half horizontally (see note)

Strawberry Red Wine Jam

8 ounces Brie cheese, cut to fit 16 sandwiches

Basil leaves (1 large or 2 small per sandwich)

FOR THE CUCUMBER GOODWITCHES:

16 Goodwitch Rolls, sliced in half horizontally (see note)

½ English cucumber, peeled and thinly sliced

1 teaspoon kosher salt, plus more as needed

½ cup cream cheese, room temperature

2 tablespoons mayonnaise

2 tablespoons fresh dill

2 tablespoons minced chives

Freshly ground black pepper

SPECIALTY TOOLS:

Toothpicks

Kitchen thermometer

TO MAKE THE ROAST BEEF GOODWITCHES: Spread the curried apricot mayonnaise on both sides of 16 sliced rolls. Fold the slice of roast beef in half lengthwise (see note). Fold it again as needed to fit the roll, giving the roast beef height. Lay the folded roast beef on the bottom half of the rolls and top with a slice of cheddar cheese. Arrange a few leaves of arugula on top of the cheese, top with the prepared top half of the roll, and skewer the sandwich with a toothpick.

TO MAKE THE BRIE AND STRAWBERRY RED WINE JAM GOODWITCHES: Spread the strawberry red wine jam over the top half of 16 sliced rolls. Cover the bottom half of the roll with Brie and top with a basil leaf or two. Cover with the prepared top of the roll and skewer with a toothpick.

TO MAKE THE CUCUMBER GOODWITCHES: Arrange the sliced cucumber in a single layer on paper towels and sprinkle with the salt. Cover with a final layer of paper towel and let rest for 15 to 30 minutes. You can stack the cucumbers by using a paper towel and salt with each layer to save space.

Combine the cream cheese, mayonnaise, dill, and chives in a bowl. Using a hand mixer or fork, mix until well combined and creamy, adding salt and pepper to taste.

Spread both sides of 16 sliced rolls with the cream cheese spread. Pat the cucumbers dry with a paper towel. Place 3 to 5 slices of the cucumber on the prepared bottom of the roll. Cover the cucumber with the top half of the roll and skewer with a toothpick.

Flower Pot Cupcakes with Rice Paper Flowers

Yield: About 24 Cupcakes | V

Some occasions—like landing in a magical new land, perhaps, and embarking on the adventure of a lifetime—call out for an extra-special treat. These three-part cupcakes are the answer to those moments and an homage to the beautifully bright flowers of Munchkinland. A moist yellow cake is the base for lemon frosting, topped with crushed pistachio "moss" or chocolate cookie crumb "dirt," and then crowned with rice paper flowers that puff before your eyes as you fry them. No Munchkins will emerge from your cupcake flower garden, but a lot of satisfied eaters will.

FOR THE CUPCAKES:

1 cup milk

3 eggs

½ teaspoon almond extract

Zest of 1 lemon

2 tablespoons lemon juice

2¼ cups flour

1¼ cups sugar

4 teaspoons baking powder

½ teaspoon salt

¾ cup unsalted butter

FOR THE RICE PAPER FLOWERS:

12 sheets rice paper

½ cup powdered sugar

½ gallon frying oil, such as peanut, safflower, soy, or canola

½ cup white chocolate chips

24 matcha Pocky sticks

FOR THE FROSTING:

1½ cups unsalted butter, cool but softened

¾ cup sweetened condensed milk

2 teaspoons fresh lemon juice

1 cup crushed pistachios or chocolate cookie crumbs (optional)

TO MAKE THE CUPCAKES: Line two 12-cup muffin pans with cupcake liners and preheat the oven to 350°F.

In a 2-cup measuring cup, measure out the 1 cup of milk. Add the eggs one at a time, whisking after each addition. Add the almond extract, lemon zest, and lemon juice and whisk again to combine.

In the bowl of a stand mixer fitted with a paddle attachment or a large mixing bowl if using a hand mixer, add the flour, sugar, baking powder, and salt. Mix to combine. Add the butter and mix on low until the mixture is a coarse crumb with most of the butter broken up into pea-size pieces.

Add all but ½ cup of the milk mixture to the flour mixture, and beat on medium speed for about 2 minutes. Scrape down the sides of the bowl, add the remaining milk mixture, and beat again for about 1 minute more.

Fill each of the cupcake liners about two-thirds full (an ice-cream scoop can help with this), and bake for 20 to 25 minutes or until a cake tester comes out clean. Allow to cool completely on a wire rack before decorating. If you are not decorating right away, store in an airtight container for up to 3 days.

TO MAKE THE RICE PAPER FLOWERS: Using the edible markers and a flower-shaped cookie cutter of your choice, trace as many flowers as you can onto each sheet of rice paper. Keep in mind that you will see the traced border color unless you choose to trim it off completely. Cut the scraps into leaves. Color the leaves and flowers as desired using the edible markers.

Place a baking rack on top of a baking sheet. Add the powdered sugar to a small strainer and place on a plate.

Add the oil to a deep fryer or Dutch oven, and place over medium-high heat. Using a fry thermometer, bring the oil up to 380°F and fry the flowers and leaves, one or two at a time. If not using a fry thermometer, test the

SPECIALTY TOOLS:

Cupcake liners

Edible ink markers

Flower-shaped cookie cutters
(simple shapes work best)

Fry or candy thermometer

✦✦✦ TIP ✦✦✦

✦ Each part of this assembled cupcake has make-ahead storage times.
Once completely assembled, the
cupcakes should be kept in a cool
place and served within 3 to 4 hours.

heat of the oil by frying a scrap of rice paper; it should start to puff the moment it hits the oil and not sink. Using metal tongs or a spider, remove the flowers and leaves from the fryer, and place on the rack to drain. Choose a "front" side, whichever you like best. Turn each item backside up and sprinkle with powdered sugar. Repeat until all the flowers and leaves have been fried. If serving within hours, you can leave them out. If making ahead, store in an airtight container for up to 3 days. They are fragile, so don't overcrowd the container.

Melt the white chocolate chips in a microwave-safe bowl in short bursts. Stir until smooth. Gently dip the top of each Pocky stick into the chocolate and "glue" it to the backside of a flower. Repeat until all the flowers have stems. Allow the stems to set for 20 to 30 minutes at room temperature or refrigerate for 15 minutes.

TO MAKE THE FROSTING: Add the butter to the bowl of a stand mixer fitted with a whisk attachment or a large mixing bowl if using a hand mixer. Whisk on high until the butter turns very pale and is the consistency of a thick spread, 3 to 4 minutes.

Scrape down the sides of the bowl. Add the condensed milk in three batches, whisking and scraping down the bowl after each addition. Add the lemon juice and mix again briefly until combined. Use the frosting immediately or store it in an airtight container at room temperature for up to 12 hours. If it needs to be stored longer, refrigerate and allow to come to room temperature before stirring and using.

TO ASSEMBLE: Use a piping bag with a large writing tip or just the ½-inch tip cut off to frost the cupcakes. Sprinkle with "moss" pistachio or "dirt" cookie crumbs, if using. Push a flower stem into the center far enough that it goes into the cake, not just the frosting, and feels stable. Add leaves where desired. Serve within a few hours.

Glinda Strawberry Jasmine Bubble Tea

Yield: 2 to 4 servings | GF, V, V+*

Glinda would definitely approve of this frothy and creamy strawberry blend, with chewy strawberry boba pearls in it—the perfect pink concoction. Remember to test the boba through your straws to make sure the pearls will fit through as your guests sip. This milk tea practically begs to be served on a tray, in a tall, cold glass—perhaps while holding a long, silver wand?

FOR THE STRAWBERRY BOBA:

½ cup chopped fresh or frozen strawberries

4 tablespoons sugar

½ cup tapioca starch, divided, plus more as needed

FOR THE STRAWBERRY MILK TEA:

2 jasmine tea bags

½ cup boiling water

2 cups fresh strawberries, hulled and sliced, or 1 cup frozen

1 cup cold milk or plant-based alternative

1 cup Cordial Munchkin Strawberry Syrup, divided (page 69)

1 teaspoon rose water

Note

This recipe is easily made vegan by using a plant-based milk option.

TO MAKE THE STRAWBERRY BOBA: Blend the strawberries and sugar in a small blender or crush well by hand. Place in a small saucepan and bring to a low boil over medium heat, pressing down on any remaining pieces of strawberry, until the sugar is dissolved, about 3 to 4 minutes. Add ¼ cup of tapioca starch to the pan, stirring with a rubber spatula until incorporated. Remove from the heat.

Turn out onto a surface lightly covered with some of the reserved tapioca. Knead, adding a small amount of tapioca at a time, until a smooth, elastic ball forms.

Cut the dough into eight pieces. Line a baking tray with parchment paper and set aside. Take one piece of dough at a time, keeping the remaining pieces covered. Using the work surface you were kneading on, roll out the tapioca dough piece into a thin rod. If the dough is cracking, run your hands under warm water and shake most of the water off. Cut one piece from the rolled dough and roll it into a ball. Test to be sure it easily passes through the straw you will be using, if applicable, knowing that the boba will expand a little as it cooks. Repeat with the rest of the dough, using your first tested piece as your guide. Arrange in a single layer on the prepared baking sheet until ready to use. If you plan to make it ahead of time, allow the boba pearls to dry for 4 hours before placing them in an airtight container for up to 1 week at room temperature, or up to 3 months in the freezer.

TO MAKE THE STRAWBERRY MILK BOBA TEA: When ready to serve, bring a medium pot of water to a boil over medium-high heat. Add the strawberry boba to the boiling water. Stir to separate the pearls, then reduce the heat to medium-low. Simmer gently, stirring occasionally, for about 20 minutes, until cooked through. Drain, rinsing the boba under cold water.

Meanwhile, make the jasmine tea by pouring the boiling water over the tea bags in a cup. Set aside to cool.

In a blender, add the strawberries, milk, tea, and 4 tablespoons of the strawberry syrup and the rose water, if using. Blend on low for 2 minutes. Taste and add more strawberry syrup, if desired.

Divide the boba among the number of servings, spooning them into the bottom of each glass. Fill the glasses with ice, then add the milk mixture. Serve with a straw and extra strawberry syrup on the side.

Cordial Munchkin Sweetness

Yield: 1 cup each basic simple syrup, cordial basil syrup, and cordial hibiscus syrup; 2 cups cordial blackberry syrup; about 1½ cups cordial strawberry syrup | GF, V, V+

Munchkinland is full of surprises, and these cordials are no exception. By using one simple base and adding blackberry, basil, strawberry, or hibiscus, you magically create different brilliant colors and flavors. These cordials are perfect for spooning into Old-Fashioned Lemonade (page 29), drizzling over fruit, or stirring into Italian soda, as your own favorite Munchkins desire.

FOR THE BASIC SIMPLE SYRUP:

1 cup sugar

1 cup water

FOR THE CORDIAL BLACKBERRY SYRUP:

2 cups fresh or frozen blackberries

1 teaspoon lemon juice

1 cup simple syrup

FOR THE CORDIAL BASIL SYRUP:

2 cups packed basil leaves

1 cup water

1 cup sugar

FOR THE CORDIAL STRAWBERRY SYRUP:

2 cups fresh or frozen sliced strawberries

1 cup simple syrup

FOR THE CORDIAL HIBISCUS SYRUP:

8 hibiscus tea bags or ¾ cup dried hibiscus flowers

1 cup simple syrup

1 tablespoon rose water (optional)

TO MAKE THE BASIC SIMPLE SYRUP: In a small saucepan, combine the sugar and water over medium heat. Stir until the sugar dissolves. Remove from the heat and allow to cool. Store refrigerated in a bottle or jar for up to 3 months.

TO MAKE THE CORDIAL BLACKBERRY SYRUP: In a medium saucepan over medium-high heat, combine the blackberries and lemon juice with the simple syrup. Simmer for 8 to 10 minutes, stirring occasionally and gently mashing the fruit as it softens. Cover and set aside for 1 hour. Strain through a fine-mesh sieve, removing the fruit and seeds, pressing down gently to remove as much liquid as possible. Store refrigerated in a bottle or jar for up to 1 week.

TO MAKE THE CORDIAL BASIL SYRUP: In a medium saucepan over medium-high heat, combine the basil, water, and sugar. Bring to a boil, stirring to dissolve the sugar. Remove from the heat and cover. Allow the basil to steep for 10 minutes. Transfer to a high-speed blender and blend on high for 3 minutes. Strain into a bowl or jar using a fine-mesh sieve, pressing down gently to remove as much liquid as possible. Cover or wrap tightly and refrigerate for up to 2 weeks.

TO MAKE THE CORDIAL STRAWBERRY SYRUP: In a medium saucepan over medium heat, combine the strawberries with the simple syrup. Once it comes to a low boil, reduce the heat to low and simmer for 20 minutes. Do not stir or press the strawberries. Strain over a bowl using a fine-mesh sieve, removing the fruit, again without pressing, which creates a cloudier syrup when working with strawberries. Cool and store refrigerated in a bottle or jar for up to 1 week.

TO MAKE THE CORDIAL HIBISCUS SYRUP: In a medium saucepan over high heat, combine the hibiscus tea bags or dried flowers with the simple syrup. Bring to a boil. Once it reaches a boil, remove the saucepan from the heat and set aside to steep for 1 hour. Strain through a fine-mesh sieve into a bowl. Stir in the rose water, if using. Pour into a bottle or jar and store in the refrigerator for up to 3 months.

HOW TO USE THE CORDIAL BLACKBERRY SYRUP:

+ Replace the simple syrup in Old-Fashioned Lemonade (page 29) with cordial blackberry syrup to make blackberry lemonade.

+ Add 1 to 2 tablespoons to a large glass with ice and seltzer to make a cordial Italian soda.

+ Add 1 tablespoon to a champagne glass and top with lemon seltzer to make a mock Kir Royale.

HOW TO USE THE CORDIAL BASIL SYRUP:

+ Use to make Wicked Lemonade (page 121).

+ Add 1 to 2 tablespoons to a large glass with ice and watermelon seltzer to make a cordial watermelon basil Italian soda.

+ Drizzle some over ice cream topped with fresh peaches.

HOW TO USE THE CORDIAL STRAWBERRY SYRUP:

+ Use the strawberry syrup to flavor the Glinda Strawberry Jasmine Bubble Tea (page 67).

+ Replace the simple syrup in Old-Fashioned Lemonade (page 29) with cordial strawberry syrup to make cordial strawberry lemonade.

+ Add 1 to 2 tablespoons to a large glass with ice and seltzer and top with whipped cream to make a cordial strawberries and cream Munchkin soda.

HOW TO USE THE CORDIAL HIBISCUS SYRUP:

+ Use to flavor the Ruby-Red Punch (page 55).

+ Spoon 2 tablespoons of hibiscus syrup and 1 tablespoon of Ginger Syrup (page 161) over ice in a large glass. Add seltzer for a delicious cordial Munchkin Italian soda.

+ To make a cordial hibiscus cream soda, add 3 to 4 tablespoons to a large glass with ice (preferably crushed). Add seltzer, leaving 2 inches at the top of the glass. Pour in 1 inch of half-and-half on top of the seltzer and serve.

Lollipop Guild Meringues

Yield: Six 5-inch lollies and 12 meringue drops | GF*, V

These homemade lollipops might not be quite as grand as the sweet presented to Dorothy by the Lollipop Guild, but they're just as tasty. Pipe your own meringues in any number of colors and flavors with a combination of extracts and food colorings, and use striped paper straws for festive sticks. Just remember that meringues will bake and harden best on a dry day—humidity is not their friend. Once you're done, wrap each lollipop in a sheet of cellophane and tie with a bright ribbon for a true Munchkinland treat.

¼ cup meringue powder

½ cup room-temperature water

1 cup fine sugar

½ teaspoon extract of choice, such as vanilla, peppermint, or lemon

6 paper straws or lollipop sticks

2 to 3 colors food coloring, such as pink, purple, and yellow

Sprinkles (optional)

SPECIALTY TOOLS:
16-inch pastry bag fitted with a large star tip

Note

This recipe is easily made gluten-free by using gluten-free sprinkles.

Preheat the oven to 175°F.

In the bowl of a stand mixer fitted with a whisk attachment or a large mixing bowl if using a hand mixer, add the meringue powder and water. Use a rubber spatula to stir gently and moisten all the meringue. Whisk until soft peaks form. With the mixer off, add ¼ cup of sugar at a time, start the mixer on low, and whisk on high for 30 seconds. Repeat until all the sugar has been added. Continue to whisk until the meringue holds stiff peaks. At this point, the mixture should feel smooth when rubbed between your fingers with no graininess. If it still feels grainy, whisk for another 30 seconds to 1 minute. Add the extract and whisk just to incorporate. Separate the meringue into three bowls, add 2 to 3 drops of food coloring, and stir to blend.

Place the pastry bag over a large glass with the top folded down and add each color, one at a time, to its own section of the bag. Use an offset spatula to push the frosting down toward the tip, flattening it along the side of the bag.

Line two baking sheets with parchment paper and use a tiny bit of meringue on each corner to hold down the parchment. Plan to space out the lollipops by placing the sticks so that the lollipop heads alternate directions. Pick up each stick, pipe a 3-inch line of meringue, and place the stick down it. Once you have placed all the sticks, pipe large rosettes over each part of the stick stuck in the meringue. Pipe 6 drops in between the lollipops on each sheet. Add sprinkles as desired, if using. Bake for 2 to 3 hours, depending on the humidity, until dry and firm to the touch. Allow to cool in the oven. Store in airtight containers, but do not stack if possible. If you need to stack them, use layers of parchment paper in between. They can be stored for 2 to 3 days.

Blueberry Basil Marshmallow Bluebirds

Yield: About 16 bluebirds | GF

As Dorothy makes her wondering way through the flowers and vines of Munchkinland, the birds twittering among the blossoms are there to greet her. You can capture a little of their sweet song with these cushiony marshmallow treats, perfect for your "We're Not in Kansas Anymore" Fruit and Edible Flower Board (page 79). Nestle them in among the fruit and flowers for a sweet finishing touch.

FOR THE BLUE SANDING SUGAR:

½ cup sugar

Blue gel food coloring

FOR THE BLUEBIRDS:

½ cup water

2 cups basil leaves

2½ teaspoons (1 envelope) unflavored gelatin

1 cup sugar

¼ cup light corn syrup

¼ cup blueberry powder, or 1.2 ounces (½ cup) freeze-dried blueberries, ground

1 teaspoon butterfly pea flower powder or 1 drop of blue gel food coloring (optional)

8 ounces blue sanding sugar

1 tablespoon chocolate chips

Nonstick oil or spray, for greasing

SPECIALTY TOOLS:

Candy thermometer

Large pastry bag fitted with a ½-inch round tip

TO MAKE THE BLUE SANDING SUGAR: Line a baking sheet with parchment paper. Preheat the oven to 200°F. Pour the sugar into the bowl of a food processor. Add 1 drop of the gel color and process for about 30 to 40 seconds. Add another drop or 2 of gel and process as needed, being careful not to add too much moisture to the sugar.

Pour the sugar mixture onto the prepared baking sheet and spread it out into an even layer (if you need to grind your freeze-dried blueberries for the bluebirds, you can do that now without needing to rinse out the bowl). Bake for 10 minutes, or until the sugar is dry. Cool the sugar for at least 15 minutes. Sift through a fine-mesh strainer to remove any clumps before using or transferring into an airtight container.

TO MAKE THE BLUEBIRDS: In a small saucepan, combine the water and the basil. Bring to a boil over high heat. Once it comes to a boil, turn off the heat, cover the pan, and let steep for at least 15 minutes or up to 1 hour. Strain the liquid into a measuring cup and throw out the basil. Measure ¼ cup of the basil liquid into the same saucepan. Pour ⅓ cup of the basil liquid into the bowl of a stand mixer. Check that the liquid has reached room temperature, placing it in the freezer for up to 5 minutes as needed. Sprinkle the gelatin evenly over the basil liquid and allow the gelatin to soften while you prepare the marshmallow mixture.

Add the sugar and corn syrup to the saucepan with the liquid and stir over medium-high heat until the sugar is dissolved. Place a candy thermometer into the sugar water and without stirring again, boil until temperature reaches the soft-ball stage (238°F). Remove the syrup from the heat.

Sprinkle the blueberry powder and the butterfly pea flower powder (or gel food coloring) over the softened gelatin in the bowl of the stand mixer or a large mixing bowl if using a hand mixer. Using the whisk attachment, beat on medium speed while slowly pouring in the syrup. Turn the speed up to high and continue beating until it is thick and glossy and the marshmallow mixture holds shape, about 8 to 10 minutes.

TO PIPE THE BLUEBIRDS: Line a baking sheet with parchment paper. Sprinkle about ¼ cup of sanding sugar evenly over the parchment paper. Transfer the marshmallow mixture to the pastry bag and wait no more than 3 to 5 minutes before beginning your first bluebird. Starting directly on the sanding sugar, pipe an oval starting and ending with the back of the bird's body. Once you complete the oval, bring the piping down the middle to the front. Go back again very slightly to create the head, then stop squeezing and jerk sharply to create the beak. Having someone ready with a sharp knife to cut the marshmallow stream will help create better beaks. If the first bluebird deflates, wait another 2 to 3 minutes before starting the next one. Sprinkle more sanding sugar all over the marshmallow bluebird, covering it completely. Repeat, working quickly, until all the marshmallow mixture has been used up or will no longer pipe. Once all your bluebirds are made, melt the chocolate chips in a small bowl in the microwave for 10 seconds. Stir with a toothpick until completely melted and use the same toothpick to paint the eyes and beaks. Cover the bluebirds with paper towels and allow to sit for at least 2 hours, or up to 1 day, to set before serving.

TO MAKE THE BLUEBIRDS USING A BIRD-SHAPED CUTTER: Lightly coat a 9-by-13-inch pan with nonstick spray or oil. Make a double batch of the Blueberry Basil Marshmallow Bluebirds. Using a lightly greased rubber spatula, spread the whipped marshmallow mixture evenly into the prepared pan. Cover loosely with paper towels. Let the marshmallow set up at room temperature for at least 2 hours. Once firm to the touch, line a baking sheet with parchment paper. Lightly grease your cutter with nonstick spray or oil and press down firmly, cutting out as many peeps as you can and greasing the cutter as needed. Coat each bluebird with the sanding sugar and set on the prepared baking sheet. Set aside to dry for another 1 to 4 hours. Serve the same day or transfer to an airtight container for up to 5 days.

Note

The marshmallow mixture gets stiff quickly, so it's better to work in single batches of this recipe if you're making the piped blue-bird version. If you're doing the cookie cutter version, go ahead and double the recipe.

Ruby Slipper Cupcakes

Yield: 12 slippers | V

The first time we see those ruby slippers poking out from under the house, we know they're special. And indeed, they shine and shimmer on Dorothy's feet for the rest of her journey. In our kitchen, they become chocolate cupcakes with ruby-red frosting. Sanding sugar, candy melts, and premade cookies help you build the slippers, which will glitter beautifully—until they're eaten.

FOR THE CUPCAKES:

1¼ cups all-purpose flour

¼ cup cornstarch

⅓ cup unsweetened cocoa powder

½ teaspoon salt

½ cup unsalted butter, softened

⅔ cup sugar

½ cup buttermilk

1½ teaspoons vanilla extract

1½ teaspoons white vinegar

¾ teaspoon baking soda

FOR THE FROSTING:

½ cup unsalted butter, softened

8 ounces cream cheese, softened

¼ cup unsweetened cocoa powder

⅛ teaspoon salt

¾ cup powdered sugar

1 teaspoon vanilla extract

2 to 3 drops red food coloring (optional)

FOR ASSEMBLY:

18 peanut-shaped peanut butter cookies

12 ounces red candy melt

About 1 cup red sanding sugar

12 oval-shaped chocolate-filled vanilla sandwich cookies

12 red, square candy fruit chews (such as Starbursts)

SPECIALTY TOOLS:

12 red-foil cupcake liners

TO MAKE THE CUPCAKES: Line a 12-cup muffin tin with cupcake liners and preheat the oven to 350°F.

In a large bowl, add the flour, cornstarch, cocoa powder, and salt. Stir to combine and set aside.

In the bowl of a stand mixer fitted with a paddle attachment or a large mixing bowl if using a hand mixer, add the butter and sugar, mix on low to combine, and then beat on high until light and fluffy, 2 to 3 minutes.

Add the flour mixture to the butter mixture in two batches, alternating with the buttermilk. Scrape down the bowl after each addition. Add the batter to the muffin liners, making sure to only fill them halfway. Bake for 20 to 25 minutes, or until a cake tester comes out clean. Allow to cool completely on a wire rack in the muffin tin.

TO MAKE THE FROSTING: In a stand mixer fitted with a whisk attachment or a large bowl if using a hand mixer, beat the butter and cream cheese together until light and fluffy, 2 to 3 minutes. Scrape down the sides of the bowl. Add the cocoa powder and salt, whisk on low to start, and then turn up to high and beat for 30 seconds. Scrape the bowl again and add the powdered sugar in three batches, scraping down the bowl between each addition. Add the vanilla and food coloring, if using, and whisk for another 30-second bursts or until well incorporated. Frost the cupcakes immediately or store in an airtight container at room temperature for up to 1 hour or store in the refrigerator for up to 1 week. Allow to come to room temperature before stirring and using.

TO ASSEMBLE: Line two baking sheets with a silicone mat or parchment paper. Use a small serrated knife to cut each peanut butter cookie in half at its narrow center. Melt half of the candy melts in a microwave-safe bowl in 30-second bursts. Stir until smooth. Take the cut cookies and make stacks of three pieces with the cut ends all facing the same direction. Spread a small bit of frosting on the top of two of the cookie pieces, gluing together in a stack, and place on the baking sheet. Repeat with the remaining stacks. Refrigerate for 10 minutes.

Add half of the remaining candy melts to the bowl and microwave in 30-second bursts, stirring until smooth. Place ½ cup of sanding sugar in a bowl with a spoon. Remove the cookie stacks from the refrigerator. Working with one at a time, spread a thin layer of the candy melt on all sides of the stack. Hold the coated stack over the bowl of sugar and spoon the sugar over it until it is covered on all sides. Place it back down on the baking sheet and spread a thin layer of candy melt on the top, and sprinkle with a bit more sanding sugar, mostly toward the back rounded edge.

Spread or pipe a bit of candy melt around the edge of each oval cookie, covering the chocolate edge, then hold over the bowl and sprinkle with sanding sugar. Refrigerate for 20 minutes to set.

While the heels and footbeds are setting, unwrap the fruit chews. Working with two or three at a time, microwave the fruit chews on a plate for 3 to 5 seconds or until just malleable. Remove from the microwave, shape into a bow, brush with a bit of water on one side, and cover in sanding sugar. Place on the second prepared baking sheet.

Frost each cupcake with a smooth layer of frosting and chill for 10 minutes. Add more sanding sugar to the bowl, remove the spoon, and gently press each cupcake into the sugar. Make sure to turn gently to coat all the edges.

Gather all the components (cupcakes stacks, oval cookies, and bows). Remelt the candy melt if needed. Press an oval cookie into the edge of one of the cupcakes while resting the other end on a stack. Use a spatula to add more candy melt between the oval cookie and the stack. Change the angle as desired by either pressing the cookie deeper into the cupcake or adding more candy melt to the back end. Serve within 3 hours.

"We're Not in Kansas Anymore" Fruit and Edible Flower Board

Yield: 12 servings; 2 cups each mango and purple berry dip | GF, V, V+*

Open up your imagination by creating this Technicolor showstopper that's just as colorful as Munchkinland. Mango and berry dips anchor a board of rainbow fruit and edible flowers arranged into fun shapes. If you want to get even more whimsical, make Blueberry Basil Marshmallow Bluebirds (page 73) to perch amid the treats. Your tasters will know they're not in Kansas anymore when they see this fruity spread.

FOR THE YELLOW MANGO DIP:

1.7 ounces freeze-dried mango (about 2 cups)

2 cups plain yogurt, preferably whole milk (see notes)

1 to 2 tablespoons honey

2 teaspoons turmeric

FOR THE PURPLE BERRY DIP:

1 cup freeze-dried blueberries

1 cup freeze-dried strawberries

2 cups plain yogurt, preferably whole milk (see notes)

2 tablespoons blueberry jam

2 tablespoons strawberry jam

FOR THE FRUIT AND EDIBLE FLOWER BOARD:

Choose from any of the following, or anything else that catches your eye (see notes):

Red: strawberries, raspberries, cherries, apples, blood oranges

Orange: apricots, papaya, peaches, cantaloupe, oranges, kumquats

Yellow: mango, pineapple, star fruit, apples

Green: grapes, kiwi, apples, pears, honeydew

Blue: blueberries, blackberries

Purple: grapes, figs, plums

Organic edible flowers: nasturtiums, borage or starflowers, chive blossoms, squash blossoms, orchids, roses, or a store-bought mix available to you (see notes)

Blueberry Basil Marshmallow Bluebirds (page 73) on toothpicks (optional)

TO MAKE THE YELLOW DIP: Place the mango in a blender. Using medium speed, grind the mango into a fine powder. Add the yogurt, 1 tablespoon of honey, and the turmeric. Blend, scraping down the sides as needed, until the color is bright and well blended. Add more honey as needed to taste. Transfer to a serving bowl, cover, and refrigerate overnight. Rinse the blender well before starting the purple dip.

TO MAKE THE PURPLE DIP: Place the blueberries and strawberries in a blender. Using medium speed, grind into a fine powder. Add the yogurt, blueberry jam, and strawberry jam. Blend, scraping down the sides as needed, until well blended. Transfer to a serving bowl, cover, and refrigerate overnight.

TO MAKE THE FRUIT AND EDIBLE FLOWER BOARD: Prepare the fruit, slicing into individual servings as needed. Place the dips onto a large platter. Arrange the larger fruits, like sliced melon, first. Layer the remaining fruits by either grouping similar colors for a rainbow theme or distributing the colors for a more whimsical look. Dot the display with the edible flowers. If using, skewer the Blueberry Basil Marshmallow Bluebirds into the fruit, allowing a little space between the peeps and the fruit to prevent them from getting soggy.

Notes

Whole milk will create a creamier dip, but you can use any plain, unsweetened traditional or plant-based yogurt.

Plan on about 12 to 18 cups of fruit, divided by how many options you choose. If you pick edible flowers from your garden, be certain they are not treated with insecticides.

This recipe is easily made vegan by choosing a plant-based yogurt and using maple syrup in place of honey.

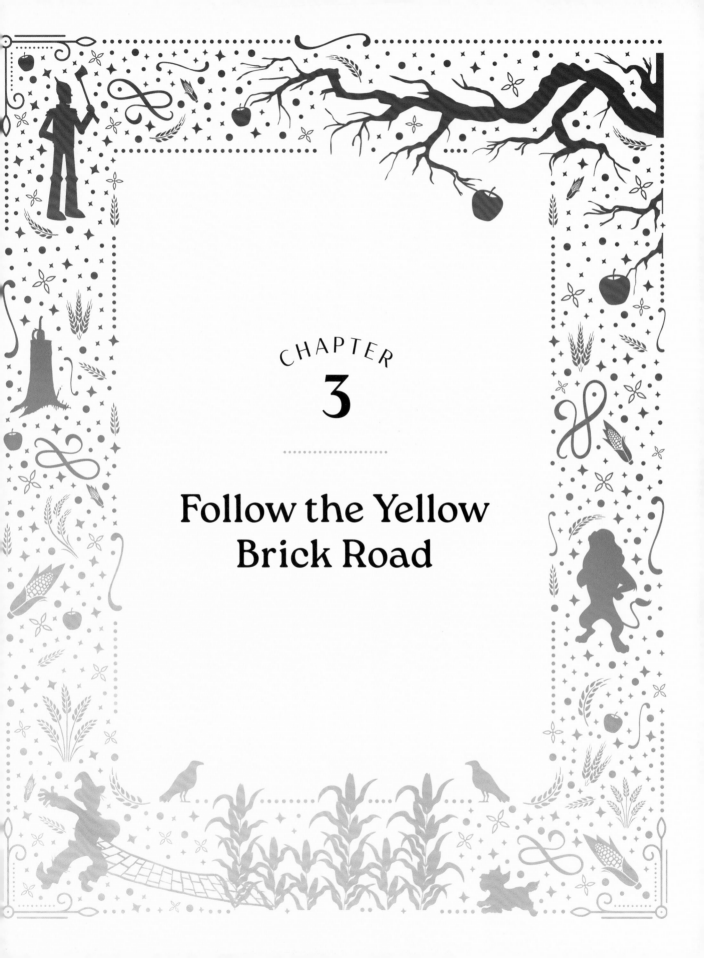

CHAPTER
3

Follow the Yellow Brick Road

Follow the Spiral Omelet

Yield: 6 servings | GF, V

All roads have to begin somewhere—and Dorothy's yellow brick road begins in the middle of Munchkinland. Your own yellow spiral starts with eggs, spinach, cream cheese, and a touch of curry powder. Rolling up your omelet creates a beautiful spiral once you cut into it. Serve this hot or cold and pair with the Emerald City Salad with Creamy Green Goddess Dressing (page 146) for an especially delicious light meal.

FOR THE OMELET:

Butter, for greasing

16 ounces frozen spinach, thawed and squeezed out

½ shallot, cut into large chunks

½ teaspoon salt

⅓ cup rice flour

1 cup heavy whipping cream

8 eggs

Freshly ground black pepper

FOR THE FILLING:

1½ cups finely shredded cheddar cheese (about 5 ounces)

8 ounces cream cheese, softened

½ teaspoon curry powder

Note

This is delicious warm or chilled. If serving warm, the filling will ooze a bit. This pairs wonderfully with Emerald City Salad with Creamy Green Goddess Dressing (page 146). All-purpose flour can be substituted for the rice flour if a gluten-free option is not wanted.

TO MAKE THE OMELET: Cover a 10-by-15-inch baking sheet with parchment paper, leaving a few inches of overhang on either end, and grease the parchment paper with the butter. Preheat the oven to 350°F.

Purée the drained spinach, shallot, and salt in a food processor until well chopped and combined. Add the rice flour and pulse until all the flour is incorporated.

In a large bowl, add the cream and eggs, one at a time, whisking after each addition. Once all the eggs are incorporated, fold in the spinach mixture. Add the pepper to taste. Spread the mixture evenly onto the prepared baking sheet.

Bake for 15 to 20 minutes or until just firm. Remove from the oven and allow to cool on the pan for 3 to 5 minutes. Run an offset spatula around the edge to loosen and use the overhanging parchment to transfer to a cutting board.

TO MAKE THE FILLING: While the omelet is baking, place the cheddar cheese and cream cheese in the bowl of a food processor and process until smooth. Add the curry powder and pulse until incorporated.

TO ASSEMBLE: Use an offset spatula to spread the filling on the omelet, keeping 1 inch at one short end clear. Starting at the filled short end, use the parchment to help lift and roll the omelet into a tight spiral. If serving, immediately remove the parchment and slice. If refrigerating, twist the parchment ends closed and transfer on the cutting board or baking sheet to the refrigerator.

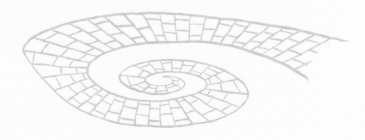

Field of Corn Polenta Bar

Yield: 8 servings | GF, V, V+*

"That's the trouble. I can't make up my mind. I haven't got a brain," the Scarecrow tells Dorothy. And with that, she's made a wonderful new friend. But your friends won't have to meet you in a field of cornstalks. Instead, bring the corn indoors and sow your table with this golden casserole of creamy polenta. For serving, arrange roasted veggies, fresh herbs, and grated cheeses in little dishes, and let your guests create their own delicious polenta bowls. No brain required.

FOR THE POLENTA:

2 ears fresh corn (optional)

6 to 8 cups water or vegetable stock, or a combination of the two, divided, plus more as needed

1 to 2 teaspoons salt (if using stock, start with 1 teaspoon)

2 cups instant polenta (see note)

FOR THE TOPPINGS BAR:

Include any or all of the following options:

3 cups cut butternut squash, cut into about 1-inch chunks

3 whole red bell peppers, halved and seeded

4 fresh corn cobs or 3 cups frozen corn kernels

Salt

2 scallions, sliced thinly on a diagonal

1 to 2 jalapeños, finely diced

2 cups cherry tomatoes, halved

1 to 2 avocados, diced

2 cups crumbled feta, cotija, or grated cheddar cheese

1 cup chopped fresh cilantro, chives, parsley, or basil

1 cup grated Parmesan cheese

TO MAKE THE POLENTA: If you are using fresh corn, use the large holes on a box grater and grate the corn down to the cobb over a large bowl, keeping all the liquid. Bring 6 cups of water or stock (8 cups if not using fresh corn) to a boil in a medium pot (see note) over medium heat. Add 1 teaspoon of salt (2 if just using water). Slowly pour in the instant polenta (see note) a little at a time, stirring constantly. Lower the heat to medium-low and stir, cooking for 5 minutes, or until the polenta begins to thicken. Add the corn with all of the liquid, if using, and cook, stirring, for another 5 minutes. Cover, take off the heat, and allow to rest for 15 minutes. If the polenta seems too thick or needs to be reheated to serve, you can stir in small amounts of water or stock over low heat to help loosen it. Taste for salt, but remember that you have some salty cheese topping options, if using.

TO MAKE THE TOPPINGS BAR: Preheat the oven to 350°F. Place the butternut squash and the peppers on a baking sheet. Bake for 40 minutes, or until tender and slightly charred, tossing once or twice. Meanwhile, cook the fresh corn cobs in a large pot of boiling salted water for 3 minutes. Drain and plunge into a bowl of ice water to stop the cooking and retain the color. Drain well. Cut the corn off the cobs. To char the corn, heat a nonstick skillet over medium heat. Add in your fresh or frozen corn kernels and stir occasionally until the kernels are nicely browned and charred on all sides. Salt to taste. Dice the roasted pepper. In separate small serving bowls, arrange the butternut squash, roasted red peppers, scallions, jalapeños, tomatoes, avocados, fresh herbs, and Parmesan.

Notes

If you are not using the recommended instant polenta, use the instructions on the box and allow for more time.

If you have a pot that works well to serve it in, use it from the start.

This recipe is easily made vegan by using vegetable stock and omitting the cheeses.

Cornstalk Cheese Straws

Yield: About 16 stalks | V

You won't need to use too much of your own brain to make Cornstalk Cheese Straws, even though they do involve puff pastry. Premade sheets make folding in the cheese, salt, and spices easy. Once your cornstalks are done, you can make them even more realistic with green food gel or edible glitter. To serve, gather them in small jars or glasses and cluster together on a tray to make a whole field of cheesy, crunchy scrumptiousness.

½ cup grated Parmesan cheese

½ teaspoon kosher salt

½ teaspoon freshly ground black pepper

¼ teaspoon garlic powder

1 sheet puff pastry, thawed

1 egg

1 tablespoon water

Green food gel or glitter (optional)

Line two baking sheets with parchment paper. In a small bowl, combine the cheese, salt, pepper, and garlic powder. Dust a work surface with about one-quarter of the cheese mixture. Place the puff pastry sheet on top of the cheese. If not completely thawed, allow to sit for another 10 minutes or so. Sprinkle 2 tablespoons of cheese mixture evenly over the short half of the puff pastry. Fold the pastry in half over the cheese mixture. Repeat by sprinkling 1 tablespoon over half and folding it again over the cheese mixture. Sprinkle another 1 tablespoon of the cheese mixture over the top. Roll the pastry back out into an 8-by-12-inch rectangle, about ⅛- to ¼-inch-thick.

Using a pizza cutter or knife, cut the pastry into about ¾-inch-thick strips along the 8-inch end of the rectangle. Using kitchen scissors or a small knife, cut about ½ inch in from the top corner of each strip about halfway in toward the center, at a sharp angle, with the cuts not meeting so the strip continues to stay intact. Continue to cut three sharp angled cuts, alternating starting points on each side and being careful not to dissect the strip at any point. Transfer to the prepared baking sheet, placing them 1 inch apart. Gently pull the "leaves" down toward the base of each stalk. Using a sharp knife, cut the uncut section of the top of each "stalk" in thin strips to create the "tassel." Use the tip of the knife to carefully pull the outer strips down slightly. Place the first tray into the refrigerator for at least 10 minutes. Set up the second tray and refrigerate for at least 10 minutes before baking.

Preheat the oven to 400°F.

Combine the egg with the water and brush the chilled cheese corn stalks with the egg wash. Bake for 8 to 12 minutes, or until puffy and golden brown. Remove from the oven and allow to cool on the baking sheet for about 10 minutes, or until firm enough to lift without bending. If using, paint green food glitter on the leaves. Serve immediately or transfer to a cooling rack.

Oh, Look! Apples and Walnut Salad with Shrub Vinaigrette

Yield: 4 to 6 servings | GF, V*, V+*

All Dorothy wants is a little snack as she and the Scarecrow skip down the Yellow Brick Road. And what could be more delicious and naturally energizing than a shiny red apple? This fruity salad is delicious, too, with the pickled apples from the apple shrub making a tangy topping. You can amp up that crunchy sweetness by glazing the walnuts with maple syrup and scattering them on a bed of onion, bacon, apples, and greens. Then drizzle with a tangy dressing incorporating the apple shrub itself. Don't worry if you don't have time to make the shrub—just substitute with apple cider vinegar and honey while making the dressing.

FOR THE VINAIGRETTE:

1 teaspoon Dijon mustard

⅓ cup apple shrub, from the Apple Shrub Mocktini recipe (page 95)

⅓ cup olive oil

¼ teaspoon salt, plus more as needed

Freshly ground black pepper

FOR THE MAPLE-GLAZED WALNUTS:

1 cup walnut halves

¼ cup maple syrup

FOR THE SALAD:

½ red onion, thinly sliced

4 slices of bacon (optional)

8 cups mixed greens, like spring mix

2 apples, cored and thinly sliced

4 cups arugula (optional)

1 cup reserved shrub apples (see note)

2 tablespoons chopped chives

TO MAKE THE VINAIGRETTE: Place the mustard and shrub in a jar with a tight-fitting lid and shake well. Add the oil, salt, and pepper, seal with the lid, and shake until emulsified. Store refrigerated for up to 1 week, shaking well before serving.

TO MAKE THE MAPLE-GLAZED WALNUTS: Preheat a medium nonstick skillet over medium-high heat. Add the walnuts and maple syrup and stir, coating the walnuts completely. Continue to cook, stirring frequently, until the walnuts have toasted, about 3 minutes. Spread out on a plate or baking sheet to cool.

TO MAKE THE SALAD: Place the sliced onion into a bowl of ice water and set aside for 10 minutes. Drain, squeezing out the extra water.

If using, arrange the bacon in a single layer on a microwave-safe plate lined with three paper towels. Cover the bacon with two more paper towels. Microwave on high for 2 to 4 minutes or until crisp, checking often to make sure it doesn't burn.

Crumble or chop the bacon. Dress the mixed lettuces with 4 tablespoons of vinaigrette. Taste, adding more vinaigrette as needed to lightly dress the lettuce. Arrange the apple slices, arugula (if using), bacon, walnuts, and onions over the lettuce and drizzle with another 1 to 2 tablespoons of vinaigrette. Sprinkle with the reserved shrub apples and chives and serve.

Notes

Save the apple drained from the shrub for a delightful pickled apple element to your salad. If you don't have time to make the shrub, substitute with ¼ cup of apple cider vinegar and 1 tablespoon of honey while making the dressing.

This recipe is easily made vegetarian or vegan by eliminating the bacon.

"She Was Hungry" Baked Apples

Yield: 6 baked apples | V

"**S**he was hungry! She was hungry!" Imagine being mocked by a tree, on an empty stomach, no less. Now imagine getting to eat one of those gorgeous apples—filled with caramel, encased in a pastry crust, and dipped in sparkling red and green sanding sugar. Arrange these beauties as a centerpiece on your table during the meal—but no throwing! They're just too pretty.

FOR THE APPLES:

¼ cup apple cider vinegar

2 tablespoons brown sugar

1 teaspoon cinnamon

6 medium to small apples

FOR THE FILLING:

¼ cup salted butter

½ cup pecans, roughly chopped

½ cup dark brown sugar

FOR THE PASTRY:

2½ cups all-purpose flour, plus more for rolling and dusting

1 tablespoon powdered sugar

1 teaspoon kosher salt

½ cup unsalted butter, very cold

¼ cup solid vegetable shortening, very cold

⅓ cup ice water

TO ASSEMBLE:

2 tablespoons milk

2 tablespoons red sanding sugar (optional)

2 teaspoons green sanding sugar (optional)

SPECIALTY TOOLS:

Apple corer or paring knife and small spoon

TO MAKE THE APPLES: In a large bowl, combine the vinegar, brown sugar, and cinnamon, and stir to dissolve the sugar.

Peel and core each apple, one at a time, and place immediately into the vinegar mixture. Turn to coat well and use a spoon to add some of the mixture into the center of the apple. Continue to peel and core each apple, adding them to the bowl and making sure to coat in the vinegar mixture. Once all the apples have been added to the bowl, set aside.

TO MAKE THE FILLING: In a microwave-safe bowl, melt the butter, then stir in the nuts and brown sugar until well combined, and set aside.

TO MAKE THE PASTRY: In a large bowl, mix together the flour, powdered sugar, and the salt. Cut the butter and shortening into tablespoon-size pieces and add to the flour mixture. Use a pastry cutter or two knives to cut the butter into the flour, creating pieces no larger than pea size. Slowly add the water a little at a time, using the pastry cutter or knives to combine. As the dough starts to form, switch to a wooden spoon or your hands to incorporate the rest of the flour into the dough, adding more water as needed.

TO ASSEMBLE: Line two rimmed baking sheets with parchment paper.

Split the pastry into six roughly equal pieces. Take one piece of dough at a time and roll it out into about a 10-inch circle. Dust with flour and smooth with your hand over the entire surface. Place an apple in the center of the circle, top-side down, and stuff the core with about 2 tablespoons of the filling.

Start to bring the pastry up the sides of the apple, much like you would a drawstring bag. Continue to bring the dough up and around the apple, smoothing it along the sides as you go and gathering the excess in your hand. Trim off the excess and flatten the remaining dough as much as possible against what will be the bottom of your apple, pinching all the seams together. Place right-side up, seam-side down on the baking sheet. Repeat with the remaining apples and pieces of pastry.

Roll the dough scraps, cut out 12 leaves, and place on the second baking sheet.

If using, place the red sanding sugar in a shallow dish. Using a pastry brush, brush each apple pastry with milk, gently roll in the sanding sugar, and replace back onto the baking sheet. Brush the pastry leaves, sprinkle the green sanding sugar on top, and replace onto the baking sheet. Refrigerate both baking sheets for 15 minutes. At the 15-minute mark, preheat the oven to 375°F.

Once the oven is preheated, bake the leaves for 7 to 10 minutes, until golden brown at the edges and crisp, then set aside to cool.

Remove the apples from the refrigerator and bake for 25 to 30 minutes or until the caramel begins to bubble and the pastry is crisp. Remove from the oven and dip the leaves into the hot caramel and attach two to the top of each apple. Allow to cool for at least 20 minutes before serving.

Once cooled completely, the baked apples can be stored in an airtight container for 2 days. They can be served at room temperature or rewarmed at 350°F for 10 minutes.

Lions and Tigers and Bear Claws, Oh My!

Yield: 12 pastries | V

Flaky, buttery bear claws are lovely when filled with almond paste and sprinkled with almonds. These delicious pastries are best served fresh from the oven. You can prep the pastries and set them up to be baked up to two days before you want to serve them. They're a perfect to-go snack if you're going on a walk in the woods . . . perhaps, a spooky woods? Filled with . . . lions and tigers and bears (oh my)!

FOR THE FILLING:

3 tablespoons unsalted butter, room temperature

½ cup brown sugar

1 cup almond flour

2 large egg whites, room temperature

1 tablespoon vanilla extract

2 teaspoons almond extract

2 tablespoons all-purpose flour

½ teaspoon salt

FOR THE BEAR CLAWS:

1 egg

1 tablespoon water

All-purpose flour, for dusting

2 sheets puff pastry, thawed overnight in the refrigerator

½ cup sliced almonds

1 cup powdered sugar

Up to 1 tablespoon milk, half-and-half, plant-based milk, or water

TO MAKE THE FILLING: Place the butter, brown sugar, almond flour, egg whites, vanilla extract, almond extract, all-purpose flour, and salt in a large bowl or the bowl of a stand mixer. Mix together with a hand mixer or the whisk attachment at low to blend the ingredients. Scrape down the sides and increase the speed to high. Beat for 4 to 5 minutes, or until fluffy, continuing to scrape down the bowl often. Transfer to a bowl, if needed, and refrigerate until needed, up to 5 days.

TO MAKE THE BEAR CLAWS: Line a baking sheet with parchment paper. In a small bowl, beat the egg with the water. Place one piece of puff pastry on a lightly floured work surface. Spread ¼ cup of the filling over half of the shorter side of the pastry. Fold the other side over the filling, being careful to match the edges. Roll the pastry out into a 9-by-12-inch rectangle. Using a pizza cutter or a knife, cut the pastry in half lengthwise, then cut each half into three even pieces. Place about 1½ teaspoons of the filling into the middle of each piece, leaving ½ inch free along all the edges. Using a pastry brush or a paper towel, brush the edges of the pastry pieces with the egg wash. Fold the pastry over the filling and press down on the edges to seal. Press down very lightly on each pastry to evenly distribute the filling, being careful not to let any escape. On the sealed end of the pastry, use a sharp knife to cut three even slits, about one-third of the way down. Fan the pastry out slightly to separate the claws. Refrigerate for at least 10 minutes while you repeat the process with the second sheet of puff pastry. If making in advance, cover with plastic wrap and store refrigerated for up to 2 days.

Remove the bear claws from the refrigerator. Brush with the remaining egg wash and sprinkle with the sliced almonds. Bake for about 15 minutes or until puffed and golden brown. Place the baking tray on a cooling rack to rest for 15 minutes. Mix the powdered sugar with the milk. Drizzle evenly over the pastries. Let the pastries sit for another 15 minutes before serving. These pastries are best baked the same day.

Apple Shrub Mocktini

Yield: 2 servings; 2 cups apple shrub | GF, V, V+

Shrubs are sweet, acidic mixers made with vinegar and fruit. We made an apple version here, inspired by one grumpy and active orchard Dorothy and the Scarecrow stumble upon. After you make your shrub, refrigerate it for up to a month. When you're ready for a refreshing mocktini, combine it with the Cordial Munchkin Sweetness (page 69) hibiscus syrup, lemon, and seltzer. You'll have a gorgeously red, appley drink to enjoy—without facing down aggressive fruit trees—and save the pickled apples to garnish your Mocktini and your Oh, Look! Apples and Walnut Salad with Shrub Vinaigrette (page 88).

FOR THE APPLE SHRUB:

2 to 3 apples, ½ inch dice (about 3 cups) (see note)

1 cup sugar

1 cup apple cider vinegar

FOR THE MOCKTINI:

2 tablespoons apple shrub

2 tablespoons Cordial Munchkin Hibiscus Syrup (page 69)

2 tablespoons lemon juice

Seltzer

Reserved apples from making the shrub (optional)

❖ Note ❖

Fuji, Gala, Honeycrisp, Envy, or Pink Lady apples all work well in this recipe. The apples can be used again after being strained and are delicious garnishing the Oh Look! Apples and Walnut Salad with Shrub Vinaigrette (page 88) or your mocktini.

TO MAKE THE SHRUB: Place the diced apples in a glass or ceramic bowl and toss well with the sugar. Add the apple cider vinegar and stir well. Seal with a lid or plastic wrap. Refrigerate for 4 to 5 days, stirring two to three times a day, making sure the sugar dissolves and the apples stay coated with the liquid.

After 4 to 5 days, strain the apples from the liquid over a bowl, pressing the apples to release as much juice as possible, reserving the apples in a separate airtight container for salads and to garnish your mocktini. The apples will keep refrigerated for 7 days. The shrub can be refrigerated for up to 1 month.

TO MAKE THE MOCKTINI: Stir 1 tablespoon of shrub, 1 tablespoon of syrup, and 1 tablespoon of lemon juice into a martini glass. Add ice and top off with seltzer. Float three pieces of the reserved apples on top and serve. Adjust the quantities to your taste and the size of your glass.

Oil Me Salad Dressing

Yield: About ½ cup or 8 servings | GF, V, V+*

I s it oil? Or is it dressing? If this tangy mixture had been in the Tin Man's oilcan, then Scarecrow and Dorothy might have just wanted to put it on a salad instead of using it to oil the Tin Man's joints. A touch of cocoa powder helps this vinaigrette masquerade as oil—until you taste it sprinkled on a green salad. It'll have you unstuck and moving in no time—just like Dorothy's favorite metallic friend.

1 clove garlic, peeled

¼ cup balsamic vinegar

¼ cup olive oil

2 teaspoons Dijon mustard

2 teaspoons black cocoa powder

1 to 2 tablespoons honey

¼ teaspoon salt, plus more as needed

¼ teaspoon pepper, plus more as needed

Place the whole garlic clove on a cutting board. Using the side of a chef's knife, gently press down on the garlic to lightly crush it. Place the garlic into a jar with a tight-fitting lid.

Add the vinegar, oil, mustard, cocoa powder, 1 tablespoon of honey, the salt, and pepper. Cover the jar with the lid and shake vigorously. Taste and add more honey, salt, and pepper as needed. Store in the refrigerator for at least 24 hours or up to 1 week. Remove the garlic and shake well before using.

Note

This recipe is easily made vegan by replacing honey with maple syrup.

If I Only Had a Heart-Shaped Ravioli

Yield: 4 servings | V*

Take heart, pasta maker, you can do this! There's no need to ask the Wizard of Oz for help with these hearts. You can make your own—and it's surprisingly easy. Get out your food processor to mix the dough and use a mini cookie cutter to press out the ravioli. You don't need to cook the pasta at once, either. Ravioli freezes well—just put the filled sheet pan in the freezer, and once frozen, place in a plastic bag. Once you're ready to cook, top your heart-shaped hard work with toasty brown butter sauce.

FOR THE RAVIOLI:

1 medium beet, or 2 small beets

1 tablespoon olive oil

2½ cups pasta flour or all-purpose flour, divided, plus more for dusting

1 large whole egg

1 to 2 large egg yolks (save one white for sealing the ravioli)

FOR THE FILLING:

8 ounces goat cheese

⅔ cup freshly grated Parmesan cheese

1 teaspoon finely minced garlic (about 1 medium clove)

¼ teaspoon kosher salt

1 egg yolk

3 tablespoons finely chopped parsley

FOR BOILING THE RAVIOLI:

4 quarts water

1½ tablespoons kosher or sea salt (see notes)

TO MAKE THE RAVIOLI: Preheat the oven to 400°F. Cut away any leafy tops close to the tops of the beet. Wash your beets well to remove any grit. Wrap one medium or two small beets together with foil and place them onto a baking sheet. Roast until fork-tender, about 40 to 60 minutes, depending on their size. Remove from the oven and set aside to cool for 10 to 20 minutes. Once cool enough to handle, grab the foil from the outside and use it to scrape the skin off the beets, using plastic gloves if you have them handy.

Place the cooked, peeled beets and the olive oil in a food processor. Pulse five times, then turn the speed up to high. Scraping down the sides as needed, continue to process for 1 to 2 minutes. Add 2 cups of flour and scrape down the sides. Process until the flour is evenly pink. Add the whole egg and 1 yolk and process until combined. Add another egg yolk as needed to create a dough that comes together and pulls away from the sides.

Turn the dough out onto a stain-resistant, floured surface. Knead with your hands until the dough is smooth and elastic, 7 to 10 minutes. Add more flour if the dough sticks to your hands or a sprinkle of water at a time if too dry or stiff. Divide the dough into two equal pieces and wrap each piece tightly in plastic. Refrigerate for at least 1 hour, or overnight. While the dough is resting, make the filling.

TO MAKE THE FILLING: Place the goat cheese, Parmesan cheese, garlic, salt, egg yolk, and parsley into a medium bowl. Using a hand mixer or a rubber spatula, mix until well combined and smooth. Cover and refrigerate until needed, or up to 3 days.

TO ASSEMBLE THE RAVIOLI: Beat the reserved egg white with 1 teaspoon of water in a small bowl. Line a baking sheet with parchment paper and dust lightly with flour. Dust a stain-resistant work surface lightly with flour. Remove one section of the dough from the refrigerator and divide it in half, rewrapping one half in the plastic to keep from drying. Using your hands or a rolling pin, flatten the dough you are starting with into a rectangle about 1 inch thick, and dust lightly with flour on both sides. Roll out into a long strip using a pasta

FOR THE SAUCE:

1 cup roughly chopped walnuts

6 tablespoons unsalted butter

2 cloves garlic, peeled and halved

¼ teaspoon kosher salt, plus more as needed

¼ teaspoon freshly ground black pepper, plus more as needed

¾ cup Parmesan cheese

⅓ cup chopped chives

SPECIALTY TOOLS:

Heart-shaped cookie cutter, in one or more sizes

Notes

Ravioli is best when boiled with-in 2 hours of assembling but will freeze well. Place the ravioli filled sheet pan into the freezer for 1 hour. Once completely frozen, you can store the ravioli in a freezer-safe container or resealable plastic bag. The pasta dough is not salted to make it easier to knead and roll, so it is important to add the full amount of salt to the water when you boil the ravioli.

This recipe is vegetarian if using vegetarian Parmesan cheese.

machine or floured rolling pin, dusting lightly with more flour as needed to prevent sticking, until slightly translucent. You should be able to almost see your fingers through the other side. If the strip becomes too long, cut it in half lengthwise and roll again. If you have cut your first piece in half and have two equal strips, begin making the ravioli. If you have one strip, repeat with the next piece of dough.

Lay the two sheets of pasta on a lightly floured work surface. Cut away any cut or torn sections and make the two sheets similar in size. Start with the sheet closest to you. Holding the cutter in the same direction for each line, very lightly mark the dough with your cookie cutter ½ inch apart, to guide where you should put the filling. You will be cutting the heart shapes out after you lay the second strip of pasta dough over the filling, so do not cut the heart out at this point. Depending on the size of your cookie cutter, using a pastry bag, mini cookie scoop, or teaspoon, place a mound of filling in the middle of each heart (about ½ teaspoon for a 1-inch heart, 1 teaspoon for a 2-inch heart, or 2 teaspoons for a 3-inch heart), leaving enough space around the edges to allow them to be sealed. Using a small pastry brush or your finger, brush the egg white wash around the perimeter of the hearts. Lay another sheet of pasta, stretching gently as needed, over the filling lined sheet. Press down gently around the filling to get rid of any air and to seal the edges. Keeping the filling in the center, press your cutter through the two layers of pasta, pulling the heart away as you lift. Use your fingers to pinch along the edges to make sure they are well sealed. Place the ravioli on the prepared baking sheet. Repeat with the remaining dough, rerolling the scraps as they accumulate.

TO MAKE THE SAUCE: Bring a large pot of water to a boil. Add the salt to the boiling water (see notes). Add the freshly made or frozen (see notes) ravioli to the boiling water. Gently stir until the water returns to a boil again. Cook the ravioli, uncovered, for 5 to 7 minutes, or until the ravioli float to the top plus another minute. Reserve 1 cup of pasta water.

While the pasta is cooking, toast the walnuts in a large, deep skillet over medium heat, stirring until they just begin to brown. Transfer to a small bowl. Cook the butter and garlic in the same pan over medium heat, stirring constantly, until the butter just begins to turn brown. Remove from the heat and stir in the walnuts, salt, and pepper. Remove the ravioli from its pot with a slotted spoon and place in the skillet with the butter sauce. Gently stir to coat. Add in ¼ cup of reserved pasta water and cook until reduced by half, 1 to 2 minutes. Remove from the heat and stir in the Parmesan cheese. Divide the ravioli and the sauce among four plates. Sprinkle with the chives and serve.

Smart Cookies!

Yield: About 36 cookies | GF, V

The Scarecrow would probably love to scarf down a handful of these tasty little cookies full of walnuts and cinnamon—both "good for the brain" ingredients. For added smarts, before baking, press a walnut half into the top of each cookie. It'll look like a little brain perched on top. Just a teaser, Scarecrow!

3 cups walnut pieces or halves, plus about 40 halves for decoration

3 large eggs, divided

¾ cup plus 1 tablespoon sugar, divided

1 tablespoon rose water (optional)

¾ teaspoon vanilla extract

1 teaspoon cinnamon, divided

Preheat the oven to 300°F. Line two baking sheets with parchment paper.

Pulse 3 cups of walnuts in a food processor until they are finely ground, being careful not to let them turn to walnut butter. Separate the eggs, placing the yolks in a medium mixing bowl and reserving the egg whites. Add the ground walnuts, ¾ cup of sugar, the rose water, vanilla, and ½ teaspoon of cinnamon and stir until well blended. Stir the remaining 1 tablespoon of sugar with the remaining ½ teaspoon of cinnamon in a small bowl. Pour one-third of the egg whites into another small bowl, reserving the remaining egg whites for another use. Roll teaspoon-size pieces of dough into balls. Dip them halfway, first into the egg white and then into the cinnamon-sugar mixture. Place 1 inch apart on the prepared baking sheets, sugar-side up. Press a walnut half into the middle of each cookie.

Bake for 16 to 20 minutes or until just lightly browned. They will continue to harden as they set, so don't be tempted to cook them longer. Remove from the oven and allow to cool on the baking sheets for at least 10 minutes. Transfer to a wire rack and allow to cool completely. Serve the same day or store the completely cooled cookies in an airtight container for up to 3 days.

I'm Losing My Hay

Yield: 8 servings | GF*, V, V+

After falling off his post in the cornfield, the Scarecrow might need a rest and a snack. Crispy, curry-seasoned hash browns are perfect, if they don't remind him too much of his own insides. Offer these alongside the Follow the Spiral Omelet (page 83) for a thoroughly Land of Oz–themed breakfast.

4 cups frozen hash browns (check for gluten-free options as needed; see note)

2 tablespoons olive oil or vegetable oil

1 teaspoon curry powder

1 teaspoon kosher salt

Preheat the oven to 400°F.

Distribute the frozen hash browns evenly over a baking sheet. Drizzle with the oil, then sprinkle with the curry and salt. Using a spatula or your hands, toss the potatoes gently to thoroughly coat. Distribute the potatoes evenly in a single layer. Bake for 35 to 45 minutes, or until very crisp, stirring often. Leave on the baking sheet until it has cooled completely before transferring to a serving bowl.

Notes

If your hash browns have frozen into big clumps, place them as is on a baking sheet in the preheated oven for 5 to 10 minutes, or until they fall apart. This will keep them from getting soggy. Once the potatoes have separated, distribute them on the baking sheet and continue to follow the recipe.

This recipe is easily made gluten-free by choosing hash browns that are labeled as gluten-free.

Cowardly Cupcakes

Yield: 24 cupcakes | V

The Cowardly Lion has nothing to fear here—the cute face on these cupcakes is his own! Brought to life with a variety of jimmies and candies, it sits on top of a hummingbird cupcake with spice frosting. Have fun gathering and arranging the decorations into proper little lions. Then have even more fun watching your guests as they enjoy your creations.

FOR THE CUPCAKES:

¾ cup unsalted butter, softened

1 cup granulated sugar

½ cup light brown sugar

3 eggs

One 8-ounce can crushed pineapple

½ cup unsweetened applesauce

1 tablespoon vanilla extract

2½ cups flour

1 teaspoon allspice

1 teaspoon baking soda

½ teaspoon salt

FOR THE FROSTING:

1½ cups unsalted butter, cool but softened

¼ cup light brown sugar

½ teaspoon allspice

¾ cup sweetened condensed milk

1 teaspoon vanilla paste

TO MAKE THE CUPCAKES: Line two 12-cup muffin tins with liners. Preheat the oven to 350°F.

In the bowl of a stand mixer fitted with a paddle attachment or a large mixing bowl if using a hand mixer, combine the butter, granulated sugar, and brown sugar. Beat on high until light and fluffy, 2 to 3 minutes. Scrape down the bowl and add the eggs one at a time, mixing after each addition. Add the pineapple, applesauce, and vanilla and mix again.

In a medium bowl, mix the flour, allspice, baking soda, and salt. Add the flour mixture in two batches to the batter mixture. Mix after each addition and scrape down the bowl to make sure all the flour is incorporated.

Fill each liner two-thirds full with batter (an ice-cream scoop works well for this). Bake for 20 to 25 minutes or until a cake tester comes out clean. Allow to cool completely before decorating. To store, place the cupcakes in an airtight container with layers of parchment if stacking. Leave at room temperature or refrigerate for up to 3 days.

TO MAKE THE FROSTING: Add the butter to the bowl of a stand mixer fitted with a whisk attachment or a large mixing bowl if using a hand mixer. Whisk on high until the butter turns very pale and is the consistency of a thick spread, 3 to 4 minutes.

Scrape down the sides of the bowl. Add the brown sugar and allspice and whisk on high for another 30 seconds.

Add the condensed milk in three batches, whisking and scraping down the bowl after each addition. Use the frosting immediately or store it in an airtight container at room temperature for up to 12 hours. If it needs to be stored longer, refrigerate and allow to come to room temperature before stirring and using.

FOR DECORATING:

1 cup sweetened shredded coconut

2 tablespoons chocolate jimmies

2 tablespoons orange jimmies

24 chocolate chips (for the nose)

48 orange candy-coated chocolates (for the cheeks)

24 heart quin sprinkles (for the tongue)

48 black candy pearls or mini chocolate chips (for the eyes)

24 candy crowns (optional)

TO DECORATE: Put a dry pan on the stove over medium-high heat and heat for 2 minutes. Turn the heat off, add the shredded coconut to the pan, and stir constantly to toast. If the coconut stops toasting, you can place the pan back over medium heat for 1 to 2 minutes, stirring continuously. Once the coconut is toasted, transfer it to a large plate and allow to cool for 3 to 5 minutes. Add the jimmies to the coconut and stir. Set aside. Gather the remaining decor pieces in small bowls and set aside.

Use an offset spatula to frost each cupcake with a smooth mound of frosting. Make a flat circle on the top of each cake by pushing some of the frosting toward the outside. This "rim" of frosting will help create the lion's mane.

Place the mini cupcake liner, upside down, over the center of a cupcake and hold the cake over the coconut mixture. Sprinkle the coconut mixture over the cake, pressing gently if needed, until the entire outer edge of the cake is coated. Carefully remove the cupcake liner and repeat with the rest of the cakes.

Place one chocolate chip, on its side, point-end down, in the center of the lower third of each cupcake. Place the orange candy coated "cheek" pieces on either side of the point and the "tongue" heart under the cheeks. Place the black candy pearls as eyes above the nose and add the crown, if using. Repeat with the remaining cupcakes. Store in a cool place for up to 12 hours or refrigerate for up to 3 days. Remove from the refrigerator at least 1 hour before serving.

I'm Feeling Chicken Liver Pâté

Yield: About 2 cups | GF

Sometimes people (and cowardly lions) might feel a little chicken about the strong taste of liver in pâté—but not with this mild, smooth preparation. Adding sharp green apples and fresh thyme helps balance the fat of the liver and cream. Spread the pâté on a baguette or crackers, or make a sandwich with pickles and mustard.

1 pound chicken livers

¾ cup milk

1 cup unsalted butter, divided

2 cloves garlic, chopped

1 small yellow onion, chopped

1 green apple, cored, peeled, and roughly chopped

1 teaspoon fresh thyme leaves, plus 1 or 2 sprigs

½ teaspoon salt, plus more as needed

½ teaspoon freshly ground pepper, plus more as needed

2 tablespoons sherry or cognac (optional)

Up to ¼ cup heavy cream

⅛ teaspoon allspice

In a small bowl, soak the livers in the milk for 20 minutes. Drain and pat dry, trimming away any connective tissue. In a medium or large skillet, melt 2 tablespoons of butter over medium heat. Add the garlic, onion, apple, thyme, salt, pepper, and sherry or cognac, if using. Cook until soft and most of the liquid has evaporated, about 15 minutes. Increase the heat to medium-high and add the chicken livers. Sauté until the livers are brown on the outside and barely pink inside, about 5 minutes. Cover, remove from the heat, and set aside for 5 minutes.

Transfer the liver mixture to a blender or food processor. Slowly add in half of the cream, the allspice, and ¾ cup of the butter, processing until smooth. Taste for salt and pepper, adjusting as needed. Add more of the cream if the mixture feels too thick, keeping in mind that the pâté will firm up as it sits overnight, processing again after each addition.

Transfer to a serving bowl or ramekins. Melt the remaining 2 tablespoons of butter and spoon a thin layer over the pâté to prevent oxidation. Refrigerate for 1 hour to set the butter layer and cover with plastic wrap. Refrigerate for at least 6 more hours or up to 3 days.

Field of Poppies Focaccia Bread

Yield: 12 to 18 servings | V*

The beautiful field of sleepy red poppies that Dorothy and her friends come across after they exit the forest inspires this savory rosemary focaccia bread. Cherry tomato halves or mini bell peppers represent the flowers, just without the sleepy effects. Add a shower of Parmesan cheese at the end for snowflakes and serve warm. This yeasty, stretchy bread will give you just enough energy to make it to Emerald City—or at least, back to the kitchen for another piece.

4 cups bread flour

1 tablespoon kosher salt

1 tablespoon instant yeast

2 cups warm water (about 110°F)

About 6 tablespoons olive oil, divided, plus more for greasing

16 to 32 mini bell peppers or cherry tomatoes

1 to 2 sprigs fresh rosemary, leaves removed

12 to 15 whole parsley leaves

2 scallions, greens only, to use as stems

2 to 4 black olives, cut into small dice, to use as poppy centers

Flaky salt

2 to 4 tablespoons Parmesan cheese (optional)

SPECIALTY TOOLS:

Kitchen thermometer

Notes

Use the tip of a knife to remove the seeds from the cherry tomato halves, if using, to prevent the bread from getting too soggy.

This recipe is vegetarian if you ensure you're using vegetarian Parmesan cheese.

In a large bowl, whisk together the flour, salt, and yeast. Using a rubber spatula, stir in the water, folding the dough until the flour is thoroughly mixed in. Cover with a greased piece of plastic wrap and let sit for 15 minutes. Move the plastic wrap to one side of the bowl and, using oiled hands, place your fingers under the side of dough farthest from you and gently lift and fold the dough in toward you. Repeat three more times, turning the bowl 90 degrees each time. Pour 2 tablespoons of olive oil over the dough. Turn the dough in the oil until it is well coated, finishing with the seam down. Cover the bowl again with the plastic wrap and place in the refrigerator for 12 to 24 hours.

Remove the dough from the refrigerator. Wet your hands with water. Place your fingers under the side of dough and once again lift and fold four times as before, ending with the seam-side down. Cover with plastic wrap and set aside for 1 hour.

About 15 minutes before baking, place a rack in the middle of the oven. Preheat the oven to 425°F. Line a 9-by-13-inch cake pan (or for thinner focaccia use two 9-by-13-inch rimmed baking sheets) with parchment paper and grease it with 2 tablespoons of olive oil. Stretch and fold the dough one more time and place the dough on the prepared baking sheet, seam-side down. Coat your hands with some of the oil. Press your fingers into the dough, spreading it out to the edges and creating deep dimples.

Cut the bottom ends off the peppers, or cut the tomatoes in half (see note), to use as the poppies. Reserve the rest of the pepper for another use, if using. Arrange the pepper ends or tomatoes, cut-side facing out, pressing them into the dimples, to create your field of poppies. Finish decorating, using the rosemary leaves and parsley as the stems and leaves. Fill the center of each poppy with a piece of black olive. Drizzle the remaining 2 tablespoons of olive oil over the focaccia and sprinkle with a pinch or two of flaky sea salt.

Bake for 25 to 30 minutes, or until golden brown. Remove the pan from the oven and sprinkle some Parmesan cheese lightly over the top half to look like snow falling. Carefully remove the focaccia from the pan onto a cooling rack. Allow to cool for at least 10 minutes before slicing.

Poppy Macarons

Yield: 10 macarons, ¾ cup chocolate ganache | V, GF

Each of these poppy macarons is shaped like one of the scarlet poppies that the Wicked Witch deviously uses to lull Dorothy to sleep—even down to the poppy seed center of each flower. Dorothy's friends could have used a plate of these to awaken her from her enchanted stupor, instead of the snow sent by Glinda—they're much more delicious and not quite as cold.

FOR THE MACARONS:

⅔ cup slivered, blanched almonds

1 cup powdered sugar

2 egg whites, room temperature

¼ cup granulated sugar

½ teaspoon almond extract

Red food coloring

1 tablespoon poppy seeds

½ cup cherry jam

FOR THE CHOCOLATE GANACHE:

½ cup dairy-free semisweet chocolate chips

6 tablespoons heavy whipping cream

1 tablespoon unsalted butter

1 teaspoon cherry syrup, from bar cherries or jam

SPECIALTY TOOLS:

2 pastry bags, one fitted with ½-inch round pastry tip and one fitted with a large petal tip, such as a 124

Note

These are best if made 1 to 2 days ahead. This allows the center to soften slightly, creating the crisp on the outside soft on the side texture of the perfect macaron.

TO MAKE THE MACARONS: Lower the oven racks to the lower third of the oven and preheat to 350°F. Line two baking sheets with parchment paper.

In the bowl of a food processor fitted with a blade attachment, process the almonds for 1 minute. Add the powdered sugar and process for 1 minute more.

Use a fine-mesh strainer over a mixing bowl and pass the almond mixture through the strainer by pushing it through with a stiff spatula. Transfer any remaining solids back to the food processor and process again for 1 minute more. Transfer back the strainer and repeat the process until 2 tablespoons or less of solids remain. Discard the solids and set the almond mixture aside.

In the bowl of a stand mixer fitted with a whisk attachment or a large mixing bowl if using a hand mixer, gently mix the egg whites and granulated sugar together on low until just combined. Raise the speed to medium-high and beat for 2 minutes, then raise the speed to high and beat 2 minutes more or until the mixture is glossy and holds stiff peaks. Add the food coloring to achieve the desired hue and the almond extract and beat for another 30 seconds.

Remove the bowl from the stand mixer and add the almond mixture all at once. Use a spatula to pull the almond mixture through the egg whites, pressing against the sides of the bowl with each stroke. This process is called *macaronage*. Do this just enough times to combine the almond mixture with the egg white. Unlike normal macarons, you want the mixture to still hold peaks when you lift the spatula up. Do not overwork or the macarons will not hold their poppy shape. We will finish the *macaronage* process to make the bottoms.

Fill the petal tip pastry bag with a little more than half the batter and use a small dot to adhere the parchment paper to the baking sheet at all four corners. With the tip nearly resting on the surface of the baking sheet, the wide part facing in toward the center, pipe the poppies by creating four heart-shaped petals in a circle. Placing the baking sheet on a cake wheel can help with this. Pipe 10 poppies, leaving 1 inch between each one.

Note: Do not tap the baking sheet! Very carefully set the sheet aside.

Work the rest of the batter a bit more with the rubber spatula, folding it until it flows like a thick batter.

Fill the second pastry bag fitted with the round tip with the rest of the batter and use a small dot to adhere the parchment paper to the second baking sheet at all four corners. With the tip about ½ inch off the surface of the baking sheet, pipe the batter into ¾-inch rounds, spacing 1 inch apart. Tap the baking sheet several times on the counter to release any air bubbles.

Bake both baking sheets for 13 to 15 minutes, rotating the sheets halfway through, until risen and just set. The poppy shaped macarons may finish 2 to 3 minutes early, so watch them carefully. Allow to cool completely on the baking sheet.

TO MAKE THE CHOCOLATE GANACHE: In a microwave-safe bowl, add the chocolate and cover with the whipping cream. Microwave for 1 minute and leave standing in the microwave for 5 minutes more. Remove from the microwave, add the butter, and stir until smooth. Add the cherry syrup and stir to incorporate. Refrigerate for 45 to 60 minutes until firm but still spreadable.

If using chocolate ganache for the macarons, place into a piping bag and pipe a circle of ganache around the edge of the bottom macaron. Fill the center of the circle with jam and top with the poppy-shaped macaron. Place a dot of ganache (or jam, if not using ganache) in the center of each poppy and press a pinch of poppy seeds onto it to cover. If not using chocolate ganache, spread or pipe a thin layer of jam on the flat side of the rounds and top with a poppy. Store refrigerated in an airtight container between layers of parchment for up to 3 days.

Mountain Climber

Yield: 2 to 4 servings | GF, V, V+

The Scarecrow, the Tin Man, and the Cowardly Lion have some tough work ahead of them when they scale the rocky mountain up to the witch's castle to save Dorothy. They might need some energy from this citrusy concoction punched up with spiced simple syrup, then served over ice. Thirsty heroic mountain climbers everywhere will thank you.

FOR THE SPICED SIMPLE SUGAR:

1 cup water

3 cinnamon sticks

4 strips orange peel

1 teaspoon whole cloves

2 pods star anise

1 teaspoon whole black peppercorns

2 bay leaves

1 cup packed brown sugar

FOR THE MOUNTAIN CLIMBER:

1 lemon, juiced

2 limes, juiced

1 cup orange juice

½ cup spiced simple syrup (½ recipe)

2 tablespoons sugar for the rim (optional)

2 to 4 strips orange peel, for garnish

TO MAKE THE SPICED SIMPLE SYRUP: In a small saucepan, combine the water, cinnamon, orange peel, cloves, star anise, black peppercorns, bay leaves, and brown sugar. Bring to a boil over high heat, stirring until the sugar has completely dissolved. Lower the heat to medium-low and simmer for 10 minutes. Remove from the heat and cover. Allow to steep for 12 to 24 hours. Strain into a small bowl using a fine-mesh strainer. Cover and refrigerate for at least 2 hours, or up to 1 month.

TO MAKE THE MOUNTAIN CLIMBER: In a shaker or a jar with a tight-fitting lid, combine the lemon juice, lime juice, and orange juice. Add the spiced syrup and shake. Wet the rims of two to four glasses with water or a cut lemon or lime. Place the sugar on a small plate. Hold the glasses upside down and press into the sugar, twisting a little to coat the rim completely. Fill the glasses with ice, shake the drink well, and pour over the ice. Garnish with a strip of orange peel and serve.

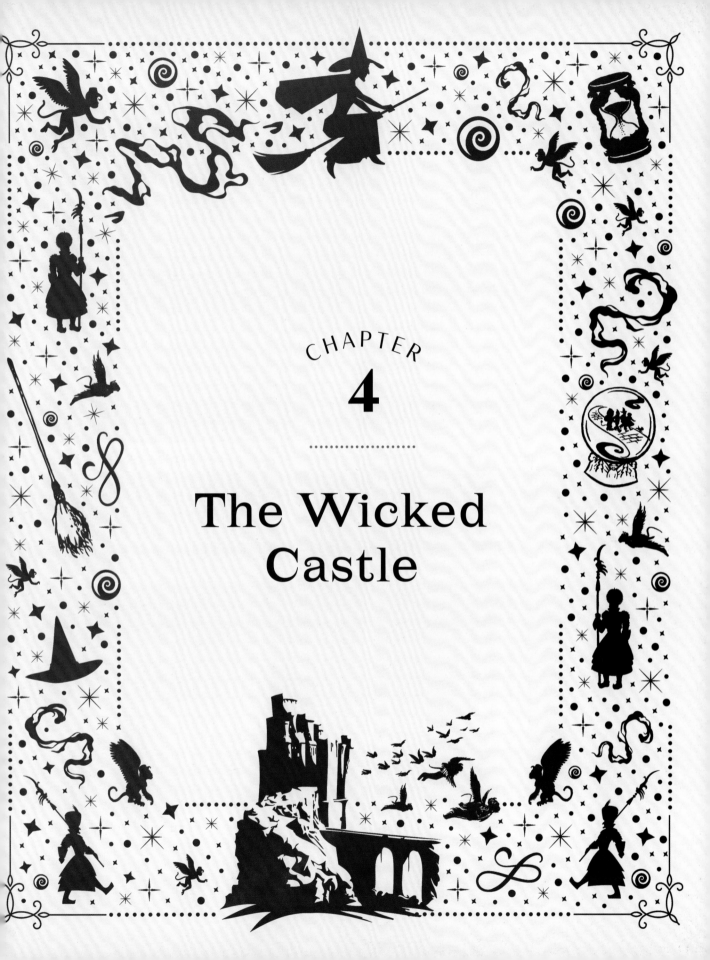

CHAPTER

4

The Wicked Castle

Bacon-Wrapped Date Winged Monkeys

Yield: 12 pieces | GF

Evil monkeys with wings may be scary, but there's nothing scary about these bacon-wrapped dates. They're the perfect sweet-smoky combo, and they look just like Winged Monkeys as you feed the skewers through the bottom of the dates and arrange them in a tall glass or vase as if they're flying on their bacon wings.

6 slices thick-cut bacon, halved

12 whole dates, pitted

SPECIALTY TOOLS:

12 toothpicks

12 skewers

Preheat the oven to 375°F.

Gently pull the ends of a piece of bacon to stretch (but without breaking it) and wrap it around the middle of a date, leaving an even amount of extra bacon on both sides, at the top, for the wings. Secure the bacon at the top of the date and under the bacon wings with a toothpick. The toothpick acts to both secure the bacon and to keep the wings spread out in flight position. Place the "monkeys" upside down onto a baking sheet, spreading the wings out flat.

Bake for about 15 minutes, or until the bacon wings are just crisp, being careful not to burn them. Remove from the baking sheet and place, still upside down, onto a second baking sheet lined with a paper towel and let rest for at least 10 minutes to crisp up.

To serve, skewer the "monkeys" through the bottom. Leaving the toothpicks in will help keep the wings in flying position. Be sure to warn your guests if they are not visible. Place the skewers into a tall narrow glass or a vase, arranging them to look as if they are flying.

Monkey Goes Bananas

Yield: 4 servings | GF, V, V+*

Being the Wicked Witch of the West's sidekick is no easy task. So, the captain of the witch's Winged Monkeys might want to sample this delicious beverage the next time he takes on an assignment. This fruity, creamy frozen drink has a banana base and kicks the flavor up a notch with strong coffee syrup and chocolate drizzles, providing even the most hardworking minions the energy needed for any mission.

FOR THE COFFEE SYRUP:

1 cup sugar

1 cup espresso, extra-strong brewed coffee, or cold brew concentrate

FOR THE LEMON-CARDAMOM SUGAR:

2 tablespoons sugar

1 teaspoon ground cardamom

Fine zest of 1 lemon

Pinch kosher salt

FOR THE MONKEY GOES BANANAS:

1 cup pineapple juice or water

About ½ cup chocolate syrup

1 banana

¼ cup coffee syrup

¼ cup spice syrup (page 113)

4 tablespoons cream of coconut (not coconut cream)

1 cup ice cubes

— Note —

This recipe is vegan if using vegan chocolate syrup.

TO MAKE THE COFFEE SYRUP: In a small saucepan over medium-high heat, combine the sugar and coffee. Bring to a boil, stirring until the sugar has completely dissolved. Lower the heat to medium-low and simmer for 3 minutes. Set aside to cool for 10 minutes before transferring the syrup into a bowl or jar. Once it has cooled completely, cover and refrigerate for at least 2 hours, or up to 1 week.

TO MAKE THE LEMON-CARDAMOM SUGAR: In a small bowl, combine the sugar, cardamom, lemon zest, and salt. Stir well, crushing a bit with the back of a spoon to release the zest oils.

TO MAKE THE MONKEY GOES BANANAS: Wet the rims of four glasses with pineapple juice or water and dip into the cardamom sugar. Drizzle chocolate syrup down the sides of the glasses, reserving about half.

Combine the banana, pineapple juice, coffee syrup, spice syrup, and cream of coconut in a blender. Blend on high until smooth. Add the ice and blend until smooth and frothy. Pour into the prepared glasses, drizzle with the remaining ¼ cup of chocolate syrup, and serve immediately.

Wicked Lemonade

Yield: 8 servings | GF, V, V+

After all that threatening and yelling at Dorothy and her friends, the Wicked Witch of the West might need to sit down with a glass of her very own Wicked Lemonade. To prepare, take yourself back to that Kansas farm kitchen with the Old-Fashioned Lemonade base (page 29), then throw in refreshing sliced cucumber and Cordial Munchkin Sweetness (page 69) basil syrup. The Wicked Witch of the West would certainly appreciate the black salt rim, too, as well as the kick from fresh jalapeño.

FOR THE WICKED LEMONADE:

2 limes, juiced, plus another wedge to salt the rim of your glass

2 cups Old-Fashioned Lemonade base (page 29)

1 teaspoon finely chopped fresh jalapeño, or more as needed

1 English cucumber, cut into large 1-inch slices

4 tablespoons Cordial Munchkin Sweetness basil syrup (page 69; optional)

4 to 6 cups cold water

FOR THE SALT RIM:

2 tablespoons black salt

2 tablespoons sugar

TO MAKE THE WICKED LEMONADE: Combine the lime juice, lemonade base, and jalapeño in a blender and process on high for about 10 seconds. Add the cucumbers and pulse until only fine chunks remain. Add the basil syrup (if using) and process for a few more seconds, leaving the cucumbers still visible. Chill for at least 2 but up to 24 hours.

TO MAKE THE SALT RIM: Combine the salt and sugar and place on a small plate slightly bigger than your serving glasses.

TO SERVE: Wet the rim of your glasses with a lime wedge. Dip each glass into the salt mix, twisting slightly, and set aside. Add the water to the cucumber lime mixture to taste, stirring, keeping the mix slightly stronger to accommodate for the ice melting in your pitcher or glasses. Pour over the ice and serve immediately in or with your prepared glasses.

My Pretty Wicked Mole with Green Polenta

Yield: 12 to 16 servings | GF

Mole is one of those dishes that just begs for a creative touch. Here, we created a spicy dark version simmered with beef brisket that would look right at home on a table in the Wicked Castle. Spoon it over a polenta for a meal as green as the witch herself. The spinach adds both freshness and color to this rich dish. Or serve the mole with Fiery Crackers (page 129) as an appetizer.

FOR THE MOLE:

5 to 6 pounds whole beef brisket

2 tablespoons kosher salt, divided (see note)

1½ tablespoons ground cinnamon

1½ tablespoons ground cumin

1 tablespoon garlic powder

1 tablespoon smoked paprika

2 tablespoons olive oil

4 cloves garlic, peeled

One 7-ounce can chipotle chiles in adobo sauce, divided

1 cup chopped prunes (about 6 ounces)

4 cups low-sodium beef or vegetable stock, divided

4 medium white onions, quartered

3 tablespoons smooth peanut, almond, or seed butter

1 tablespoon unsweetened cocoa powder

2 tablespoons unsweetened black cocoa powder (or increase the regular cocoa powder to 2 tablespoons)

⅓ cup black garlic, finely chopped

TO MAKE THE MOLE: Pat the brisket dry with paper towels. Sprinkle all sides of the brisket liberally with 1 tablespoon of salt.

Combine the cinnamon, cumin, garlic powder, and smoked paprika in a small bowl. Season the brisket liberally with half of the spice mixture, reserving the remaining spice mixture for the sauce. Proceed to the next step or cover and refrigerate for up to 24 hours.

Preheat the oven to 250°F.

Heat the oil in a large Dutch oven or stockpot over high heat. Using tongs, sear the brisket for 10 minutes on both sides, starting with the fattier side.

Place the reserved cinnamon seasoning blend, 1 teaspoon of kosher salt, the garlic, two chipotle chiles, and the prunes in a blender or food processor. Pulse five to seven times. Add 2 cups of stock and blend for 1 minute on low speed. Add the onions in two batches, pulsing two or three times, or until the onions are finely chopped.

Pour the sauce over the seared meat, using the tongs to make sure the sauce is evenly distributed. Add more stock as needed to just cover the brisket, saving the remaining stock to use as needed during the cooking process. Cover with a lid and cook over medium-low heat for 10 minutes. Place into the preheated oven. Cook for 1 hour per pound, checking every 2 hours, adding more stock as needed to keep the meat just barely submerged. Remove from the oven and let sit for 1 hour, or allow to cool and refrigerate overnight.

Gently remove the brisket from the braising liquid onto a cutting board. Spoon off some of the fat floating at the top of the sauce. Stir in the nut butter, cocoa powder, black cocoa powder, and the black garlic. Add salt and the reserved adobo sauce to taste.

Slice the brisket against the grain and place into the sauce. Keep warm over low heat for up to 30 minutes. Serve warm with polenta.

FOR THE GREEN POLENTA:

3 cups water, plus more as needed

4 cloves garlic, peeled

1 pound frozen chopped spinach

4 cups vegetable stock or water

2 teaspoons salt, plus more as needed

2 cups instant polenta (see note)

¼ cup olive oil

½ to 1 cup grated Parmesan cheese (optional)

Notes

How much salt is needed will depend on how salty your stock is and your personal taste. Start slowly and add more at the end as needed.

If you are not using instant polenta, follow the cooking directions on the package, adding in the puréed spinach at the end.

TO MAKE THE GREEN POLENTA: In a medium pot, bring the water and garlic to a boil over medium-high heat. Boil for 5 minutes. Add the frozen spinach and bring back to a boil, stirring. Drain the spinach and garlic over a bowl. Return the liquid from the drained spinach to the pot and add the vegetable stock. Bring to a boil. Slowly stir in the polenta, making sure no clumps form. Reduce heat to medium-low and cook, stirring, for 5 minutes. Cover, remove from the heat, and allow to sit for 15 minutes.

Place the cooked spinach and the garlic in a blender or food processor. Add the olive oil and purée until smooth, adding 1 tablespoon of water at a time as needed to achieve a smooth paste.

Stir the spinach mix into the cooked polenta. Return to medium-low heat and reheat, stirring, for about 5 minutes, or until the polenta has thickened slightly, adjusting the salt to taste as needed. The polenta will continue to thicken as it sits, so it can be a bit loose at this stage. The Parmesan cheese can be stirred in at this point or offered on the side.

What a World Sphere

Yield: 4 servings | GF*, V

"What a world! What a world!" the Wicked Witch wails as she melts to the floor of her castle in a cloud of steam. You can capture a bit of this classic scene with our own version—chocolate "world" spheres, matching cookie brooms, and a warm chocolate sauce that melts the spheres in real time, all served over ice cream. Sphere molds will help create 3D chocolate "worlds" but you can also make a 2D disk version that's equally tasty.

FOR THE SPHERES AND BROOMS:

4 ounces semisweet chocolate

Green petal dust (optional)

4 chocolate candy chews (such as Tootsie Rolls)

4 rolled wafer cookies

FOR THE ESPRESSO CHOCOLATE SAUCE:

2 tablespoons instant espresso

2 tablespoons water

1 tablespoon vanilla extract

¾ cup heavy whipping cream

4 ounces semisweet chocolate, chips or chopped small

4 ounces milk chocolate, chips or chopped small

1 pint ice cream, such as vanilla, mocha, or chocolate

SPECIALTY TOOLS:

3-inch silicone sphere mold

Notes

If you don't have a sphere mold, you can line a baking sheet with parchment and use an offset spatula to spread the chocolate into four disks.

Serve the ice cream in a dish or glass just smaller than the disks and set the disks on top.

This recipe can be made gluten-free by using gluten-free cookies or omitting the brooms.

TO MAKE THE SPHERES AND BROOMS: Add 3 ounces of chocolate to a microwave-safe bowl and heat it in two 30-second bursts, stirring between each time. Add the remaining 1 ounce of chocolate and continue stirring until smooth. Use the retained heat as much as possible and only microwave again in 10- to 20-second bursts if needed.

Set the sphere mold on a small cutting board or baking sheet and use a pastry brush to coat the inside of each cavity with the melted chocolate. As the chocolate cools in the mold, continue to brush it up the sides to make sure the chocolate is all the way to the edges and not too thick on the bottom. Once the mold is completely coated, refrigerate for 10 minutes.

While the spheres are setting, make the brooms. Place the chocolate chews on a microwave-safe plate and heat for 5 to 10 seconds, until just pliable. Gently press and stretch each chew into a rough square, about 2 inches by 2 inches. Cut a thin strip off each square, about ⅛-inch wide, and set aside. Working with a short side, fold over a ⅛-inch strip on each piece. Use kitchen shears to cut strips into each piece, all the way across, about ⅛ inch wide. Do not cut past the fold, creating a curtain. Wrap a wafer-cookie end with the candy chew, about 1 inch up from the bottom, and press the ends together to seal. Just below the end of the cookie, cinch the "broom" bristles with one of the candy strips you set aside. Repeat until you have created four brooms.

Gently unmold the spheres. Use a dry pastry brush to dust with petal dust, if using. Serve immediately or store in a cool place in a single layer in an airtight container for up to 3 days.

TO MAKE THE CHOCOLATE SAUCE: In a microwave-safe bowl, add the instant espresso and water. Heat for 30 seconds and then stir until the espresso is dissolved. Add the vanilla and heavy cream. Stir to combine and add the semisweet and milk chocolates. Microwave for 1 minute and let stand in the microwave for 5 minutes. Whisk until smooth. This can be served immediately or stored in an airtight container in the refrigerator for up to 1 week. To serve after storing, microwave in short bursts, stirring in between each one.

TO ASSEMBLE: Place a scoop of ice cream in a small dish or on a small plate, and top with a chocolate sphere and broom. Have the warmed sauce in a serving pitcher or individual pouring vessels for each guest. Pour the sauce over the sphere to reveal the ice cream.

Wicked *Cruel*-lers

Yield: About 12 to 15 *cruel*-lers | V

A wicked version of Auntie Em's Crullers (page 11), these darkly delicious *cruel*-lers get their rich flavor from butter, cocoa powder, and a chocolate glaze, with green pistachios adding crunch. Make the dough for your wicked delights a day ahead of time, but fry them up as close to serving as possible. You will need parchment paper and a pastry bag fitted with a large star tip for this variation of a classic cruller.

FOR THE *CRUEL*-LERS:

1¼ cups all-purpose flour

¼ cup black cocoa powder or regular cocoa powder (see note)

1 tablespoon pumpkin pie spice (see note)

½ cup milk

½ cup water

4 ounces unsalted butter, cut into cubes

3 tablespoons sugar

½ teaspoon salt

4 large eggs, divided

6 cups vegetable oil, for frying

Notes

Black cocoa powder will give you dark, wicked-looking *cruel*-lers. The pumpkin pie spice deepens the flavor, hinting of gingerbread. If you don't like the taste of dark chocolate, choose a cocoa powder with 20 percent or higher cocoa fat for a smoother chocolate taste, and skip the pumpkin pie spice.

TO MAKE THE *CRUEL*-LERS: Sift the flour, cocoa powder, and pumpkin pie spice together and set aside. Place the milk, water, butter, sugar, and salt in a medium, heavy-bottomed saucepan over medium heat. Stir with a wooden spoon or rubber spatula and bring to a boil. Turn off the heat immediately and add all of the flour mixture. Stir vigorously until well combined. When all of the flour has been absorbed, place over medium heat and stir constantly for about 2 minutes, or until the dough pulls away from the sides and is smooth. Transfer the dough into a large bowl and set aside until the dough is just warm to the touch and no longer hot, about 10 to 15 minutes (set your timer). Whisk one of the eggs in a small bowl. Add the whisked egg into the bowl with the dough and stir until thoroughly incorporated. Repeat with the remaining 3 eggs. Place a piece of plastic wrap directly on the surface of the dough and refrigerate for at least 1 hour, or up to 24 hours.

While the dough is chilling, cut parchment paper into fifteen 4-inch squares. Using a round glass or cutter, draw a 2½- to 3-inch circle in the middle of one of the squares to use as a template. Using a rubber spatula, place some of the dough into the pastry bag, filling it no more than two-thirds of the way. Place another parchment square over the traced circle to use as your guide. Evenly pipe the dough, overlapping the ends, to create the circle. Repeat until you have used up all the dough, refilling the pastry bag as needed. Let the *cruel*-lers sit, uncovered, while you heat the oil.

Line a baking sheet with paper towels and place a wire rack on top of the paper towels. In a deep, heavy-bottomed pan or Dutch oven, add the oil until it is about 3 inches deep. Heat until 375°F. Working with one parchment square, carefully pick up the *cruel*-ler and place it gently, face down, into the hot oil with the paper still attached. Once it detaches itself, after about 10 seconds, remove the paper with tongs. Allow the *cruel*-ler to continue frying until slightly puffed and cooked through, about 2 minutes on each side, using tongs to gently turn them. Transfer to the wire rack. Working with one square at a time, continue by adding up to two or three *cruel*-lers to the oil, depending on your comfort level and the size of the pan. Allow the fried *cruel*-lers to sit for 15 minutes before glazing.

FOR THE CHOCOLATE GLAZE:

5 tablespoons unsalted butter

6 tablespoons cocoa powder

1 cup powdered sugar

2 teaspoons vanilla extract

1 tablespoon hot water, divided

TO DECORATE THE *CRUEL*-LERS:

½ cup shelled raw pistachios, chopped

SPECIALTY TOOLS:

Kitchen thermometer

TO MAKE THE CHOCOLATE GLAZE: In a small saucepan over medium-low heat, stir the butter with the cocoa powder for 5 minutes. Stir in the sugar and vanilla. Adding 1 teaspoon of the hot water at a time, stir until the glaze is smooth and thick.

TO DECORATE THE *CRUEL*-LERS: Dip the warm or room-temperature *cruel*-lers in the glaze. Place back on the wire rack, glazed-side up, and immediately sprinkle with about ½ tablespoon of the chopped pistachios. Continue with the remaining crullers. Let the glaze set for about 15 minutes. Serve immediately if possible, or the same day.

Fiery Crackers

Yield: 10 servings | V, V+*

Spicy, garlicky, and smoky, these marinated soda crackers lob a fireball's worth of flavor, with aim even better than the Wicked Witch's. They're even more delicious when dipped in Wicked Hummus (page 141) or My Pretty Wicked Mole with Green Polenta (page 122). Don't be afraid of the amount of olive oil this recipe calls for. It will help the crackers maintain their fiery flavor and coating.

1 teaspoon garlic powder

1 teaspoon ground cumin

1½ tablespoons red pepper flakes

1 teaspoon smoked paprika

½ teaspoon kosher salt

Freshly ground black pepper

1 cup olive oil (see note)

8 ounces soda crackers

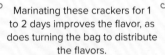

Notes

Marinating these crackers for 1 to 2 days improves the flavor, as does turning the bag to distribute the flavors.

If you are planning to marinate chicken or steak in the near future, save the bag and reuse it. Just add some fresh garlic, salt, and more black pepper to stretch out all those good seasonings.

This recipe is easily made vegan by choosing a vegan cracker.

Place the garlic powder, cumin, red pepper flakes, smoked paprika, and salt into a large 1 gallon resealable bag. Add several grinds of freshly ground pepper and the olive oil. Seal the bag and swirl these ingredients until well mixed. Place all the crackers into the bag and gently turn the bag two to three times. Place on a counter, shaking to spread out the crackers in the bag. Turn the bag over every 5 minutes for 30 minutes. Allow the crackers to marinate for 12 to 48 hours (see note), turning the bag over and shaking it gently often.

Preheat the oven to 250°F. Line one large baking sheet with parchment paper. Arrange the crackers in a single layer on the baking sheet, saving the bag for another use (see note). Bake until the crackers are lightly browned, 15 to 20 minutes. Allow to cool completely. Serve or store in an airtight container for up to 1 week at room temperature.

Wicked Black Bread

Yield: 1 loaf (12 to 16 slices) | V, V+

White bread would somehow look out of place in the Wicked Castle, so we like to make our Badwitches (page 133) with this yeasty black bread instead. It's perfect for soaking up melty Brie and chocolate. Later, toast the leftovers and spread the slices with butter and jam. Black cocoa and espresso color the loaves a deep brown—like pumpernickel but without the rye.

3½ to 4 cups bread flour, divided, plus more for dusting

3 tablespoons brown sugar

3 tablespoons black cocoa powder

1 teaspoon instant espresso or coffee powder (see note)

2¼ teaspoons instant yeast (1 package)

1⅛ cups water

2 tablespoons apple cider vinegar

2 tablespoons salted butter, room temperature

1 teaspoon fine salt (see note)

Oil, for greasing

SPECIALTY TOOLS:
Kitchen thermometer

Notes

If using unsalted butter, increase the salt to 1¼ teaspoons.

If you don't have instant espresso or coffee on hand, use 1⅛ cups of strong coffee instead of the water, making sure the temperature does not exceed 110°F when adding it to the flour mixture.

In a large mixing bowl, whisk together 2½ cups of flour, the brown sugar, cocoa powder, espresso, and yeast. Set aside.

Place the water, vinegar, butter, and salt into a microwave-safe measuring cup or bowl. Microwave on high, in 30-second intervals, until the liquid reaches about 110°F. Remove from the microwave and stir.

Using a rubber spatula, stir the water mixture into the flour mixture. Continue sprinkling the flour over the dough ¼ cup at a time, folding into the dough with the spatula after each addition, until a sticky dough forms. Turn the dough onto a floured surface and knead the dough with your hands until smooth and still slightly tacky, sprinkling in more flour as needed.

Lightly grease a large bowl with the oil. Place the dough in the bowl, turning it to coat it with the oil. Cover the bowl with an oiled piece of plastic wrap. Place in a warm, draft-free spot until the dough doubles in size, about 1 hour.

After the first rise, shape the dough into an oblong loaf. Place into a greased 9-by-5-inch bread pan and cover loosely with greased plastic wrap (you can reuse the same piece). Set aside to rise for about 1 hour, or until doubled.

Meanwhile, preheat the oven to 375°F. If you have a spray bottle, uncover the dough and spray the top of the loaf lightly with water to help get the best rise. Bake for 35 to 40 minutes, or until the internal temperature reaches 200°F. If you don't have a thermometer, remove the loaf from the pan and tap the bottom to make sure it makes a hollow sound. If not yet making a hollow sound, return the bread to the pan and bake for 5-minute intervals as needed. Transfer the loaf to a wire rack and allow it to cool completely before slicing.

Badwitches

Yield: 4 to 8 servings | V

A wicked take on the Festive Munchkin Goodwitches (page 61), these Badwitches are oozing with melted Brie and chocolate, with the crisp toasted bread providing a wonderful crunch. Bright green basil scattered across the top contrasts beautifully with the Wicked Black Bread (page 130). Run, Toto, run—right out of the castle and straight for a plate of these. You'll thank us, little dog.

4 slices Wicked Black Bread (page 130)

4 tablespoons blackberry jam

2 tablespoons semisweet chocolate chips

6 ounces Brie cheese, sliced

½ cup slivered or chopped basil

Preheat the oven to 350°F.

Place the bread on a baking sheet. Place the baking sheet into the oven and toast the bread for about 4 minutes, turning the slices over once after about 2 minutes. Remove the baking sheet from the oven but leave the oven on. Spread 1 tablespoon of jam on each of the bread slices. Sprinkle the chocolate chips lightly over the jam. Divide the Brie evenly, arranging it in a single layer over the chocolate. Place the baking sheet back in the oven and bake for 3 to 4 minutes, or until the Brie starts to melt. Remove from the oven and gently spread the Brie evenly across the bread. Allow to sit for 5 minutes. Sprinkle with the basil, cut into squares or triangles, and serve.

Wicked Crystal Ball Shaker Cookies

Yield: 6 to 8 shaker cookies | V

Enter the Wicked Witch of the West's castle with this black-and-green version of Professor Marvel's Crystal Ball Cookies (page 32). Color the dough dark brown with cocoa powder, then ice the cookies in green and black. Luckily, peering into these crystal balls will only bring up visions of the delicious treat you and your guests are about to enjoy.

FOR THE DOUGH:

¾ cup salted butter, softened

4 ounces cream cheese, softened

¾ cup firmly packed light brown sugar

½ cup black cocoa powder

1 egg

1 teaspoon vanilla extract

2¾ cups all-purpose flour, plus more for dusting

About 6 ounces precooked isomalt pieces

Green luster dust (optional)

FOR THE ICING:

4 cups powdered sugar, sifted

3 tablespoons meringue powder

6 tablespoons water

½ teaspoon peppermint extract (optional)

1 to 2 drops black and bright green food coloring

TO ASSEMBLE THE SHAKER COOKIES:

Sprinkles, such as flowers, green jimmies, and/or red nonpareils

Green sanding sugar

SPECIALTY TOOLS:

5-inch-tall snow globe cookie cutter

2½-inch circle cookie cutter

3 pastry bags with writing tips

Edible markers

TO MAKE THE DOUGH: In a large bowl, beat together the butter, cream cheese, brown sugar, and cocoa until light and fluffy. Add the egg and vanilla and beat again until well combined. Add the flour 1 cup at a time, mixing on low and mixing by hand with the last ¾ cup.

Split the dough in half, form into disks, wrap in parchment paper, and chill for at least 1 hour. Toward the end of the hour, preheat the oven to 375°F.

Place the isomalt crystals in a resealable bag and crush into smaller pieces, no larger than a pea. Place in a resealable container, cover, and set aside. Line two baking sheets with silicone mats or parchment paper.

After chilling the dough, work with one half at a time on a lightly floured silicone mat or work surface. Roll out each disk to ⅛ inch thick and cut out as many snow globes as you can with the cookie cutter (you will need three snow globes for each shaker cookie). From the center of two of the globes in each set, cut a circle with the circle cookie cutter. Remove the circle shape and use them for another purpose (such as clock faces for the Be Still, My Ticking Heart Cookies [page 158) or reroll with the scraps to make more globes. Place the cookies on the prepared baking sheets and chill for 15 minutes.

Bake for 3 minutes. After 3 minutes, remove the cookies from the oven and place crushed isomalt in the center hole of one of each set, making sure it goes from edge to edge but does not stick up too much past the dough. Return to the oven and bake for another 7 to 9 minutes or until just starting to brown at the edges and the isomalt is completely melted. Remove from the oven and give the cookie sheet a few firm taps on a cutting board to release some of the bubbles from the isomalt. Allow to cool completely on the baking sheet, about 15 minutes.

Repeat with the second disk of dough.

TO MAKE THE ICING: In the bowl of a stand mixer fitted with the whisk attachment or a large bowl if using a hand mixer, combine the powdered sugar, meringue powder, water, and peppermint extract, if using. Whisk on low speed for 7 to 10 minutes, or until the icing holds stiff peaks (if using a hand mixer, whisk on high speed for 10 to 12 minutes).

✦ ✦ ✦ Tips ✦ ✦ ✦

✦ Precooked isomalt is available online or at craft stores and specialty baking stores. It is very easy to work with and holds up well without absorbing moisture. You can substitute crushed hard candy for the shaker window, but you will need to keep the cookies in an airtight container as soon as possible; they will last about 24 hours before the window begins to collapse.

✦ If possible, roll out the dough directly onto a silicone baking mat, use the cookie cutters as directed, and remove the scraps of dough from the mat, rather than moving the cut out cookies. This will help the cookies keep their shape and match up well when assembled together.

✦ If you don't want to make shaker cookies, use the markers, sugar, and icing to create your scene on the crystal ball directly on the crystal ball shapes.

Divide the icing into three small bowls and use the food coloring to create your desired colors. Transfer the icing to pastry bags fitted with writing tips. Keep some icing white for glue or other decorations you may want to add.

TO DECORATE AND ASSEMBLE: Use a small pastry brush dipped in a bit of water to spread a bit of the bright green icing onto the center of the intact snow globe (this will be the background to your scene). Allow to dry completely, 20 to 30 minutes. Take the center cookie, the one without the isomalt window, and pipe some icing "glue" all along the backside, including on the base, leaving a ¼-inch border along the inside window edge. Gently press this spacer cookie onto the base cookie. Add your sprinkles to the center. At this time, if desired, color the window by brushing a small amount of luster dust evenly over the back side of the isomalt window. Add your icing glue in the same way to the window cookie and gently press onto the assembled cookies creating the completed stack of three. Do not move until completely dry, 30 minutes to 1 hour. Once dry, you can use a bit of icing and your damp pastry brush to coat the outside of the cookies and sprinkle with sanding sugar to complete the illusion of a crystal ball. Decorate the base of the crystal ball as desired with the black icing. Allow to dry completely.

Store in an airtight container or seal each shaker cookie in a treat bag.

"I'm Melting" Matcha Ice Cream with Hat Topper

Yield: About 2 pints ice cream and 6 hats | GF*, V

When at last the Wicked Witch is vanquished, she melts into a pile of robes, with Dorothy, her friends, and the guards all watching. In our recipe, the iconic cry of "I'm melting!" isn't such a bad thing—we have homemade green matcha ice cream sitting (meltingly) at a circle of witch's-robes ganache, and, of course, a pointy ice-cream cone hat sitting atop the delicious heap. Eat it right away or invite your tasters to let it melt in homage to our favorite Wicked Witch.

FOR THE ICE CREAM:

2½ cups heavy whipping cream

2 tablespoons matcha powder

1 teaspoon vanilla paste or
2 teaspoons vanilla extract

¼ teaspoon spirulina powder
(optional)

One 14-ounce can sweetened
condensed milk

FOR THE WITCH HATS:

6 ounces bittersweet chocolate,
broken into small pieces

6 ginger cookies, about 3 inches
in diameter

6 chocolate ice-cream cones

½ cup heavy whipping cream

Notes

If you can't find chocolate ice-cream cones, use sugar cones and dust them using 2 teaspoons of black cocoa powder and a pastry brush before adhering to the cookies.

This recipe can be made gluten-free by using gluten-free cookies and cones.

TO MAKE THE ICE CREAM: Add the cream, matcha, vanilla paste, and spirulina (if using) to the bowl of a stand mixer fitted with a whisk attachment or a large mixing bowl if using a hand mixer. Whisk on low until the ingredients are combined, and then mix on high until stiff peaks form. Gently fold in the sweetened condensed milk until no streaks of it remain. Pour into an airtight container and let sit in the freezer overnight, but for at least 6 hours.

TO MAKE THE WITCH HATS: Line a baking sheet with either a silicone mat or parchment paper.

In a microwave-safe bowl, melt 4½ ounces of chocolate in 30-second bursts, stirring in between. When the chocolate is mostly melted, remove from the microwave, add the remaining 1½ ounces of chocolate, and continue to stir until all the chocolate is melted.

Dip the top of each ginger cookie into the chocolate, lift and shake off the excess, place chocolate-side up on the prepared baking sheet, and immediately top with a cone. The cones can be jaunty in placement and angle. Allow to set for 15 to 20 minutes.

Once you have dipped all the cookies, make the ganache by adding the whipping cream to the chocolate and stir until smooth. Cover and set aside until serving.

TO ASSEMBLE: Spoon about 2 tablespoons of the ganache onto a plate, spreading out into an organic circle. Place a large scoop of ice cream in the center of the circle, top with a hat, and serve.

The hats can be made up to a day ahead, placed in an airtight container until ready to serve. Refrigerate the chocolate ganache in an airtight container and gently microwave until spoonable when ready to serve.

Savory Wicked Crepe Cake

Yield: 12 servings | V

For a wicked spin on the Over the Rainbow Crepe Cake (page 41), find your inner Wicked Witch of the West with this savory crepe cake. No rainbows this time—instead, dark chocolate crepes are layered with a garlicky blue cheese filling. Spoon caramelized pear compote over the top and scatter with maple-glazed walnuts. Make this cake up to two days in advance and store the compote and walnuts separately. Then assemble just before serving, and watch your eaters fall helplessly under your spell.

FOR THE CARAMELIZED PEAR COMPOTE:

6 tablespoons salted butter

¾ cup sugar

1 cinnamon stick

8 black peppercorns

1 bay leaf

2 tablespoons lemon juice

5 large Bartlett pears, cut into about ½-inch cubes

2 tablespoons red or white wine or water, plus more as needed

FOR THE MAPLE WALNUTS:

1 cup walnuts

¼ cup maple syrup

Flaky salt

FOR THE CHOCOLATE CREPES:

2 cups whole milk

4 large eggs

4 ounces butter, melted, divided

¾ teaspoon salt

⅓ cup sugar

⅓ cup black cocoa powder

1 cup all-purpose flour or gluten-free flour

TO MAKE THE CARAMELIZED PEAR COMPOTE: Melt the butter in a large skillet over medium-low heat. Stir in the sugar. Increase the heat to medium and continue to cook until the mixture turns a light caramel color, stirring frequently.

Add the cinnamon stick, peppercorns, bay leaf, lemon juice, pears, and wine. Continue cooking, stirring gently, until the pears are tender and the juices begin to thicken. Add more wine or water 1 tablespoon at a time if the sugar mixture seizes up. Continue to cook until the liquid thickens and becomes sticky, coating the spoon. Remove the cinnamon stick, peppercorns, and bay leaf. Transfer the compote to a serving bowl and set aside to cool. The cooled pears can be made in advance and stored in an airtight container in the refrigerator for up to 1 week.

TO MAKE THE MAPLE WALNUTS: Heat a small nonstick pan over medium heat. Toast the walnuts until you start to smell the toasted aroma, about 5 minutes. Pour in the maple syrup and cook, stirring often, until most of the maple syrup has been absorbed by the walnuts, about 5 minutes. Sprinkle a pinch or two of salt over the walnuts and continue to cook, stirring, until the maple syrup crystallizes on the walnuts. Allow to cool on a plate. Once cooled, the walnuts can be stored in an airtight container for up to 1 week.

TO MAKE THE CHOCOLATE CREPES: Place the milk, eggs, 4 tablespoons plus 1 teaspoon of melted butter, the salt, sugar, cocoa powder, and flour into a blender. Start on low to blend. Scraping down the sides, increase the speed to medium, blending until smooth. Allow the batter to sit for at least 15 minutes at room temperature or up to 24 hours in the refrigerator, ideally overnight to blend the flavors. Blend again just before using to make the crepes.

Line a large plate or baking sheet with parchment paper. Heat a 6- or 8-inch nonstick skillet or crepe pan over medium heat. Using a silicone pastry brush, a crumpled piece of paper towel, or the cut side of a small halved potato, brush a small amount of the reserved melted butter over the pan's surface. Using a ladle or ¼-cup measuring cup, pour about 3 tablespoons of the batter into the hot pan to create a thin circle, swirling the pan to make each crepe about 6 inches and as evenly round as possible.

FOR THE HERBED BLUE CHEESE FILLING:

One 8-ounce package cream cheese, softened

1 cup crumbled blue cheese

¼ cup finely chopped chives

¼ cup finely chopped parsley

1 green onion, trimmed and finely chopped

2 cloves garlic, crushed or very finely minced

1 tablespoon dried dill

½ teaspoon kosher salt

½ cup sour cream or Greek yogurt

½ teaspoon freshly ground black pepper

FOR THE POACHED PEAR WITCH'S HAT (OPTIONAL):

1 small Bartlett pear

1 cup red or white wine, apple cider, or water

¼ cup sugar

2 to 3 drops black or green food coloring (optional)

Note

As you make your crepes, keep the one you are most proud of for the top layer. Use any broken or slightly smaller crepes for the center layers.

Cook the crepe for about 30 to 60 seconds, or until the edges just begin to crisp. Turn the crepes onto the prepared plate or baking sheet, stacking them on top of one another without any worry at this point of how they land. Do not worry about crepes that break or look uneven. They can still be used for the middle layers.

Continue making the crepes until all the batter is used. If you make one you are especially proud of, set it aside on another plate to use as the top layer. Set the next best one aside for the bottom. Allow the crepes to cool completely.

TO MAKE THE HERBED BLUE CHEESE FILLING: Combine the cream cheese, blue cheese, chives, parsley, green onion, garlic, dill, salt, sour cream, and black pepper in the bowl of a stand mixer or large mixing bowl if using a hand mixer. Using the whisk attachment or hand mixer, beat until creamy, scraping down the sides often. Keep at room temperature if you are using within about 15 minutes, or transfer into an airtight container and refrigerate for up to 3 days. Bring back to room temperature before assembling the crepes.

TO ASSEMBLE: Layer the first crepe on the base of an 8-inch springform pan (see note) or large serving plate. Making sure the cream cheese filling is room temperature and spreadable, use the back of a fork or a rubber spatula and carefully spread a thin layer of the filling over the crepe. Place another crepe over the cream cheese spread and continue until all the crepes or cream cheese have been used. Broken crepes can be alternated with whole crepes and pieced together as you assemble.

If using a springform pan, attach the outside ring, cover with plastic wrap, and refrigerate overnight or up to 2 days. If using a plate, place the finished crepe cake into the freezer for 10 minutes (set a timer to help you remember) to let it set up to prevent shifting. Wrap completely in plastic wrap and refrigerate overnight, or up to 2 days.

TO MAKE THE POACHED PEAR WITCH'S HAT: Check that your pear fits inside a 2-cup microwave-safe measuring cup or tall bowl so that the liquid has room to cover the pear completely. Combine the wine with the sugar into the measuring cup or bowl and microwave on high for 3 minutes, stirring occasionally, or until the sugar has completely dissolved. Stir in the food coloring, if using. Peel the pear while leaving the stem intact. Place the pear into the liquid, making sure it is completely submerged. Place a very small hole in the middle of a sheet of plastic wrap that is large enough to cover the measuring cup. Place the hole over the stem and seal. Repeat with another piece of plastic wrap to help hold the pear upright. Microwave on high for about 3 to 4 minutes, until the pear is just tender when pierced with a skewer. When the pear is tender, allow it to remain in the liquid until it cools completely. Proceed, or refrigerate in the liquid for up to 2 days.

When ready to serve, slice the pear just along the bottom to help it stand up straight. With a small paring knife, core the bottom third of the pear from the bottom. Starting about ¼ of the way up, slice down into ½-inch slices, all the way around the pear, keeping the pear otherwise intact. Arrange the sliced sections of the pear in a circle around the top portion of the pear. Place on top of the crepe cake. Serve the savory crepe cake with the pear compote and glazed walnuts.

Wicked Hummus

Yield: 2 cups of each color | GF, V, V+*

Featuring both black and green versions, this hummus duo looks much more appealing than the Wicked Witch of the West does, especially when plated side by side in the same bowl. Black sesame seeds and a handful of green herbs provide color as well as flavor. Offer Fiery Crackers (page 129) for dipping for a wicked trifecta.

FOR THE BLACK HUMMUS:

1 cup black sesame seeds

6 tablespoons olive oil, divided

2 teaspoons kosher salt, divided

1 tablespoon honey

10 cloves black garlic, roughly chopped (see note)

One 15-ounce can chickpeas, drained, reserving the liquid

¼ cup lemon juice

2 to 4 teaspoons black cocoa (optional; see note)

FOR THE GREEN HUMMUS:

1 cup loosely packed basil leaves

½ cup parsley, leaves and tender stems

½ cup cilantro (optional)

¼ cup roughly chopped chives

1 green onion, trimmed and cut into 4 pieces

2 cloves garlic, peeled and minced or smashed

4 tablespoons olive oil

Juice of 1 lemon, divided

One 15 ounce can chickpeas, drained, reserving the liquid

½ cup tahini

Salt

TO MAKE THE BLACK HUMMUS: Toast the black sesame seeds in a large pan over low heat for 1 to 2 minutes, stirring with a wooden spoon until you just begin to smell the toasted sesame aroma. Remove from the heat and allow to cool for 10 minutes.

Add the toasted sesame seeds to a high-powered food processor or blender and pulse until ground. Add 3 tablespoons of olive oil and ½ teaspoon of salt. Add the honey and black garlic. Scrape down the sides and pulse again three or four times.

Add the chickpeas, lemon juice, and 1 teaspoon of salt and blend for 1 to 2 minutes until the mixture is smooth. Add 2 tablespoons of the reserved chickpea liquid and the remaining 3 tablespoons of olive oil. Blend on high speed until you reach your desired consistency, adding more chickpea liquid or cold water as needed. If you have black cocoa powder and want a richer dark color, add 1 teaspoon at a time, blending well after each addition. Add the remaining ½ teaspoon of salt to taste.

TO MAKE THE GREEN HUMMUS: Add the basil, parsley, cilantro, chives, green onion, and garlic to a blender or bowl of a food processor. Pulse three or four times. Add the olive oil and 3 tablespoons of lemon juice. Process on low until a coarse paste forms, scraping down the sides. Add the chickpeas and tahini and process on high speed until smooth, adding the reserved chickpea liquid 1 tablespoon at a time as needed. Add salt and more lemon juice to taste. Refrigerate for at least 2 hours to help settle the flavors, or for up to 3 days.

Serve immediately or store for up to 3 days in the refrigerator in an airtight container.

Notes

Black cocoa and black garlic deepen the color and flavor of this recipe. We use these ingredients in several of our more wicked recipes.

This recipe can easily be made vegan by using maple syrup in place of honey.

Don't forget to save any leftover aquafaba (chickpea liquid) to make the Fuzzy Mitten (page 157).

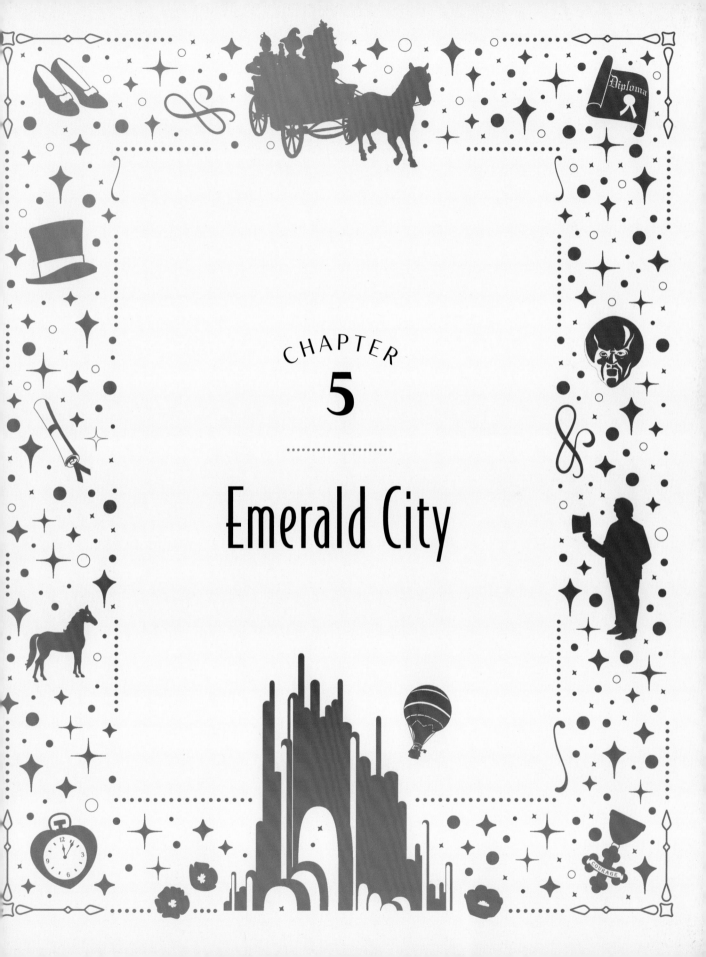

CHAPTER
5

Emerald City

Emerald City Quiche

Yield: 6 to 8 servings | GF*, V

Whoever said you can't eat your dreams? Nosh on the Emerald City and the poppy-strewn road leading up to it by re-creating the iconic scene on this sunny-yellow quiche. Bright green asparagus stalks are your emerald spires, and red and yellow peppers stand in for the poppies and the yellow brick road. Cut your prep time by using a premade piecrust or mix up Tried and True Piecrust (page 22). Then you're off to see the wonderful Wizard of Oz.

½ recipe Tried and True Pie Crust (page 22), or store-bought pastry shell

1 pound medium-size asparagus stalks (about 20 stalks)

4 eggs

1½ cups half-and-half

1 teaspoon onion powder

1 teaspoon kosher salt

Freshly ground black pepper

1½ cups cheese (shredded cheddar, mozzarella, Gouda, crumbled feta, or a combination)

1 yellow mini bell pepper

6 to 8 red mini bell peppers

1 pitted black olive

Note

This recipe is easily made gluten-free by using a 1-to-1 gluten-free flour.

Line a pie pan with the pie dough. Gently press the dough into the plate. Trim the crust, leaving a ½-inch overhang. To make a fluted edge, fold the overhang under along the edge. Use the index finger of your dominant hand to press out along the edge, from the inside of the pie. Use your thumb and index finger of your other hand to pinch around the dominant finger from the outside. Continue around the entire edge. Place the pie plate in the freezer while you begin the filling. Alternatively, use a store-bought pastry shell.

Preheat the oven to 375°F. Cover the dough with a piece of parchment paper and fill with pie weights, dry beans, or sugar. Blind bake for 12 minutes. Carefully remove the pie weights. Prick holes all over the bottom of the crust with a fork and bake again for another 5 to 7 minutes. Remove from the oven, but leave the oven on.

Meanwhile, bring a large pot of water to a boil over high heat. Blanch the asparagus for 1 minute. Drain and plunge into a bowl of ice water. Drain well, placing the asparagus upright into a colander. Cut 12 to 15 pieces of asparagus of various thicknesses into various lengths for the Emerald City skyline. Cut all the remaining asparagus into ½-inch pieces.

In a medium bowl, whisk the eggs, half-and-half, onion powder, salt, and black pepper. Stir in the cheese(s).

Place the asparagus pieces into the prebaked pie shell. Place in the oven for 3 minutes. Pour the egg mixture over the asparagus. Use the reserved asparagus stems to create the Emerald City skyline, staggering the lengths. Cut the yellow bell pepper into bricks for the Yellow Brick Road. Cut the bottom ends off the red bell peppers and place cut-side up for the poppies. Cut the olive into squares for the center of the poppies.

Place the quiche onto a baking sheet and put into the oven. Bake for 35 to 45 minutes, or until set and the top begins to color. Remove from the oven and allow to rest for at least 15 minutes before slicing. Serve warm or room temperature.

★ Emerald City Salad with Creamy Green Goddess Dressing

Yield: 8 to 12 servings; 1½ cups dressing | GF, V*, V+*

As green as the Emerald City itself, this crunchy salad is delicious as prepared below but is also the perfect recipe for improvisation. Mix in your own favorite green veggies, then drizzle with the wonderful umami-rich green goddess dressing chock-full of fresh herbs. Don't worry if you're not an anchovy fan. Just omit and increase the amount of capers.

FOR THE DRESSING:

2 anchovy fillets (see note)

1 teaspoon capers

1 tablespoon caper juice

3 tablespoons fresh lemon juice, divided

1 tablespoon Dijon mustard

1 cup packed fresh parsley

½ cup packed fresh basil leaves

2 tablespoons fresh tarragon leaves
or 2 teaspoons dried tarragon

¼ cup chives or scallions greens

⅓ cup mayonnaise

⅓ cup sour cream, Greek yogurt, or vegan substitute

½ avocado

½ teaspoon fine sea salt, plus more as needed

½ teaspoon freshly ground black pepper, plus more as needed

FOR THE SALAD:

1 handful fresh haricots verts (French green beans)

4 green onions

12 cups mixed salad greens, mixing or matching spring mix, arugula, baby kale, or spinach

1 cup Persian cucumber, thinly sliced on an angle

1 cup thinly sliced fennel

1 cup pea shoots or other microgreens

1 cup edamame beans

1 cup snap peas, left whole or sliced on a diagonal

1 avocado, cubed

TO MAKE THE DRESSING: Add the anchovy fillets, capers, caper juice, 2 tablespoons of lemon juice, and the mustard to the bowl of a food processor or blender. Pulse two or three times until the anchovy is chopped.

Add the parsley, basil, tarragon, and chives and pulse again, scraping down the sides, until a paste forms. Add the mayonnaise, sour cream, and avocado and process until smooth, scraping down the sides and adding salt and pepper to taste. Add the remaining 1 tablespoon of lemon juice if you want a tangier dressing and blend again until smooth.

Refrigerate for at least 2 hours to settle the flavors. Store in an airtight container in the refrigerator for up to 5 days.

TO ASSEMBLE THE SALAD: Bring a medium pot of water to a boil over medium-high heat. Add the green beans and boil for 1 minute. Drain and rinse thoroughly and quickly submerge in an ice bath. Drain and set aside to dry on paper towels.

Take the green onions and remove the white bottom third and reserve for another use. Slice the light and dark green of the onions. Gently mix the greens together in a serving bowl or on a deep platter. Arrange the cucumber, fennel, pea shoots, edamame, snap peas, and avocado on top and serve with the green goddess dressing on the side or toss with the salad before serving.

Notes

To make the dressing vegetarian, or if you're not a fan of anchovy, omit and increase the amount of capers to 1 tablespoon.

This recipe is easily made vegan by choosing a vegan mayonnaise and using capers in place of the anchovies, as suggested.

Emerald City Pistachio Cake with Glass Pears

Yield: 8 to 10 servings | GF, V

Gleaming green, the Wizard of Oz's castle in Emerald City is the answer to Dorothy's wishes—at least she hopes it is. Our pistachio cake captures a little of the wizard's glamour with a green sponge cake and delicate candied glass pears. And this cake holds a secret, too, though not a man behind a satin curtain—it's gluten-free, using almond flour and pistachios instead of wheat flour.

FOR THE GLASS PEARS:

2 cups water

2 cups sugar

3 to 4 drops green gel food coloring, plus more for painting

¼ cup white balsamic vinegar

6 plus pears, divided, plus more as needed

TO MAKE THE GLASS PEARS: Line two baking sheets with either a silicone baking mat or parchment paper. Set aside. Preheat the oven to 325°F.

In a large deep skillet over medium-high heat, bring the water to a low simmer, add the sugar, and continue to simmer until all the sugar is dissolved, stirring frequently. Once the sugar is completely dissolved, add the food coloring.

Place the vinegar in a large bowl.

Starting with one or two pears, begin slicing them about ⅛ inch thick from top to bottom on the mandoline. The first one or two slices will be mostly

FOR THE PEAR COMPOTE:

2 cups diced pears (about 2 pears or the leftovers from above)

2 tablespoons unsalted butter

¼ cup pear syrup (from the glass pears)

1 teaspoon ground ginger

FOR THE CAKE:

¼ cup milk

¼ cup sour cream

1 cup unsalted pistachios, roasted

6 eggs, separated

1 cup sugar

2½ cups blanched almond flour (not almond meal)

1 tablespoon baking powder

⅛ teaspoon salt

FOR THE FROSTING:

9 ounces good-quality white chocolate or 1½ cups good-quality white chocolate chips

8 ounces cream cheese, softened

4 ounces Chevre goat cheese, softened

¾ cup unsalted butter

1½ tablespoons reserved pear syrup

SPECIALTY TOOLS:

Mandoline or very sharp knife

skin and can be discarded. If using a mandoline, you may want to slice until you reach the core, then switch sides and slice from that direction. Any pieces you don't like the shape of, as well as the center of the pear, should be added to the vinegar. The pear slices to be candied (the prettiest slices) should be added to the syrup until the pan is full in a single layer. Simmer the slices for 4 to 6 minutes, or until very tender and beginning to become translucent. Use tongs to remove the slices to the prepared baking sheet. Turn off the heat under the syrup.

Remove about ¼ cup of syrup from the pan into a heatproof glass or mug and add a few more drops of food coloring. Use the tongs to dip each pear slice into the syrup and place it back on the baking sheet. Bake for 15 minutes, turn over, and bake for 10 to 15 minutes more or until almost completely dry. Use tongs to move the pear slices to a wire rack to cool completely.

While the first batch of pears is baking, turn the heat back on under the syrup and repeat the process with another one or two pears. Reserve the pear syrup in an airtight container and refrigerate until needed.

Once the glass pears are cool, they should be stored in an airtight container between layers of parchment paper until ready to serve.

TO MAKE THE PEAR COMPOTE: When you have baked two sets of pear slices, peel and dice the pear pieces you added to the vinegar and the remaining pears, returning the pieces to the vinegar as you go. You should have about 2 cups of diced pears when you are through. Set aside.

In a large skillet (it can be the same as above) over medium heat, melt the butter. When the butter begins to foam add the pears and cook for 3 to 5 minutes until the vinegar has evaporated. Add ¼ cup of the syrup and simmer, stirring occasionally, for 8 to 10 minutes. The pears should be just tender but still have a bit of crunch. Remove from the heat and allow to cool completely. Store in an airtight container in the refrigerator until ready to serve.

TO MAKE THE CAKE: Line the bottom of two 8-inch cake pans with a round of parchment paper. Preheat the oven to 350°F.

In a medium bowl, combine the milk and sour cream and stir until well blended. In the bowl of a food processor, pulse the pistachios until they are a fine texture, like coarse sand. Add the pistachios to the milk mixture and stir to combine. Set aside.

In the bowl of a stand mixer fitted with a whisk attachment or a large bowl if using a hand mixer, add the egg yolks and sugar. Whisk on high until the mixture is pale in color and almost doubled in volume, 3 to 5 minutes. Add the almond flour and the baking powder and stir to combine but do not overmix. Add the pistachio mixture and stir until just combined.

Add the egg whites to the clean bowl of a stand mixer fitted with a whisk attachment or a clean large bowl if using a hand mixer. Beat the egg whites on medium-low until just foamy, add the salt, and then mix on high until stiff peaks form. Gently fold one-third of the egg whites at a time into the pistachio mixture. Continue to fold in until all the egg whites have been incorporated and no white streaks are visible. Be gentle while folding in the egg white to maintain

If the goat cheese is too over the rainbow for you, substitute with an additional 4 ounces of cream cheese.

The glass pears, syrup, and compote can be made up to 3 days ahead of serving.

The crumb of this gluten-free cake is very delicate, which makes it delicious but a bit fragile. Move the cake layers with a large bench scraper or spatulas to avoid breaking them.

as much volume as possible. Split the batter evenly between the two cake pans and bake for 15 to 20 minutes or until a cake tester comes out clean. Allow to cool in the pan for 15 minutes before removing from the pan to a cooling rack.

TO MAKE THE FROSTING: In a microwave-safe bowl, melt the white chocolate gently, 30 seconds at a time. Stir between each time until completely smooth. Set aside.

In the bowl of a stand mixer fitted with a whisk attachment or a large bowl if using a hand mixer, beat the cream cheese and goat cheese together until light and fluffy. Slowly add the white chocolate, about one-quarter at a time, whisking on low for 10 to 15 seconds and then turning up to medium-high until incorporated. Repeat until all the white chocolate has been added.

Cut the butter into tablespoon-size pieces and, with the mixer running on medium, add one piece at a time until all the butter has been added. Add the syrup and whisk on medium-high for about 30 seconds. Use immediately or store in an airtight container in the refrigerator for up to 1 week. It is very important that the frosting be brought back up to room temperature before stirring or using.

TO ASSEMBLE THE CAKE: Remove the pear compote from the refrigerator and allow to come to room temperature.

Place one of the cake layers on a serving plate. Frost with about ¾ cup of frosting. Use an offset spatula to press some of the frosting to the outside edge all around the cake, creating a low "wall" the whole way around. Fill the center with the pear compote. Place the second layer on top. Frost the top and sides of the cake using an offset spatula to smooth. Refrigerate for at least 30 minutes before serving or up to 24 hours. If the cake has been made ahead, remove from the refrigerator at least 30 minutes before serving. Decorate with the glass pears just before serving.

Honor Rolls

Yield: 8 rolls

Your eaters will be as pleased as the Scarecrow receiving his diploma when you serve these tiny "diplomas" filled with cream cheese and salmon, a classic brain food. Slice up English cucumbers to add crunch, then offer the trimmed ends of the rolls to your helpers as snacks rather than letting them go to waste.

FOR THE CREAMY HERB CHEESE SPREAD:

8 ounces cream cheese, room temperature

½ teaspoon garlic powder

½ teaspoon dried dill

½ teaspoon dried parsley

Salt

Freshly ground black pepper

FOR THE HONOR ROLLS:

Four 7- to 8-inch flour tortillas

8 ounces creamy herb cheese spread

8 ounces sliced smoked salmon

1 English cucumber, peeled and thinly sliced

Chives, for the ties

TO MAKE THE CREAMY HERB CHEESE SPREAD: Combine the cream cheese, garlic powder, dill, and parsley in a medium bowl. Using a hand mixer or a rubber spatula, mix thoroughly. Add salt and pepper to taste. This can be stored in an airtight container for up to 1 week. Bring the spread to room temperature to assemble the rolls.

TO MAKE THE HONOR ROLLS: Cut each tortilla in half. Spread a thin layer of the herb spread over the entire surface of each tortilla half. Start at the long, cut side of the tortilla, leaving about ½ inch free, and place a single layer of the salmon and then cucumber, leaving the top 1½ inches free. Tightly roll the cut edge toward the round edge. Press down on the seam to seal. Continue using the remaining ingredients. Continue to wrap each roll individually and refrigerate overnight.

Before serving, cut about ½ inch off the ends of each roll, serving the tasty-but-not-so-pretty pieces as snacks to helpers. Choose 8 thicker chives, wrap them in a damp paper towel and microwave for 5 to 7 seconds. Tie them around the middle of each roll, knotting gently and as tightly as possible without tearing. Trim the chives with scissors as needed.

A Pie of a Different Color

Yield: 16 servings | V

Slab pies are a great way to size up your dessert if you're serving a crowd. This one uses summer fruits, but you can swap out peaches, cherries, and plums for fall and winter fruits like apples, pears, and cranberries. To keep some of that many-colored magic, try to use three different-colored fruits when you can. Then you can laugh the day away, too, in your own kitchen, rolling out piecrust and spreading jam.

FOR THE FILLING:

6 tablespoons unsalted butter, room temperature

½ cup brown sugar

1 cup almond flour

2 large eggs, room temperature

1 tablespoon vanilla extract

1 teaspoon almond extract (optional)

2 tablespoons all-purpose or gluten-free 1-to-1 flour

½ teaspoon salt

FOR THE SLAB PIE:

1 recipe Tried and True Pie Crust (page 22) or store-bought double crust

6 medium peaches or 16 medium apricots, sliced

2 pints strawberries, sliced

2 pints blueberries

½ cup apricot jam

1 egg yolk (optional)

1 teaspoon water (optional)

TO MAKE THE FILLING: Place the butter, brown sugar, almond flour, eggs, vanilla, almond extract (if using), flour, and salt in a large bowl or the bowl of a stand mixer. Mix together with a hand mixer or your whisk attachment at low speed to blend the ingredients. Scrape down the sides and increase the speed to high. Beat for 4 to 5 minutes or until fluffy, continuing to scrape down the bowl often. Use immediately or store, covered, for up to 3 days in the refrigerator. Allow to come back to room temperature before proceeding.

TO MAKE THE SLAB PIE: Preheat the oven to 375°F.

Roll the piecrust out into a 13-by-19-inch rectangle. Transfer the dough to an 11-by-17-inch rimmed baking sheet or jelly roll pan, leaving 1 inch hanging over each side, untrimmed. Spread the filling evenly over the crust. Arrange the peaches on one-third of the pie, then the strawberries on the next third, and fill in the remaining third with the blueberries. Warm the jam in the microwave for 30 seconds, or until slightly runny. Using a pastry brush or the back of a spoon, coat the fruit evenly with the jam. Fold in the pastry edges and crimp with your fingers. If using, mix the egg yolk and water in a small bowl and brush the mixture over the exposed crust edges. Bake for 35 minutes. Remove from the oven and loosely cover the edges with foil. Continue baking for another 15 minutes. Remove the pie from the oven and set on a wire rack. Remove the foil and let cool for 1 hour before serving.

Fuzzy Mitten

Yield: 4 to 6 servings; 3 cups pistachio milk | GF, V, V+*

The Wizard of Oz's guards can't fall asleep during their shifts. This green shaken tea drink has just enough caffeine to keep them awake, and it even matches the color of their uniforms. The pistachio milk and aquafaba—reserved liquid from a can of chickpeas—keeps this recipe vegan as well as light and foamy.

FOR THE CREAMY PISTACHIO MILK (OPTIONAL):

1 cup dry pistachio nuts

Salt

2 to 4 tablespoons honey or maple syrup (optional)

FOR THE FUZZY MITTEN:

4 tablespoons aquafaba (reserved chickpea liquid)

2 tablespoons sugar

2 teaspoons matcha powder, sifted

2 cups creamy pistachio milk or other preferred milk

Note

This recipe is vegan if using maple syrup and pistachio or other dairy-free milk.

TO MAKE THE CREAMY PISTACHIO MILK: Soak the pistachios in a bowl for 6 to 12 hours, covered, in the refrigerator. Drain well. Place into a high-speed blender and pulse until roughly chopped. Add 2 cups of water and blend on high until smooth. Add the salt and honey to taste. Blend again for another minute. Using a fine-mesh strainer or nut bag, strain into a jar or bottle and refrigerate until ready to use, for up to 5 days.

TO MAKE THE FUZZY MITTEN: Using a hand mixer or a whisk, beat the aquafaba in a medium to large bowl until fluffy and thick, 6 to 7 minutes. Sprinkle in the sugar and continue beating until a firm peak is reached. Add the sifted matcha powder and beat again until well incorporated, scraping down the sides as needed.

Fill four 12-ounce or six 8-ounce glasses halfway with ice. Distribute the milk into your glasses until three-quarters full. Dollop the whipped matcha over the milk, add a spoon or straw, and serve immediately.

Be Still, My Ticking Heart Cookies

Yield: About 12 cookies | V

Sugar cookie dough, heart-shaped cookie cutters, and a few different food colorings are all we need to bring the Tin Man's ticking heart to life in our own kitchens. To get truly fancy, add a watch chain made of red licorice, then decorate your hearts using gold sanding sugar and gold luster dust. These cookies are delicate, so store them in a single layer and handle with care.

One recipe Professor Marvel's Crystal Ball Cookies and icing (page 32)

2 to 3 drops cinnamon oil or ¼ teaspoon cinnamon extract (add to the icing while beating; optional)

Black edible marker

Red gel food coloring

Yellow gel food coloring

Gold sanding sugar

White sanding sugar

Gold luster dust (optional)

FOR THE CHAIN (OPTIONAL):

12 candy licorice vines

SPECIALTY TOOLS:

4-inch heart-shaped cookie cutter

2½-inch round cookie cutter

Mini (1-inch) flower cookie cutter (optional)

Wooden chopsticks (optional)

Pastry bag with writing tip

Notes

To easily coat the chain in luster dust, find a long shallow container with a lid that will fit the chain. Add about ¼ cup of nonpareils and ¼ teaspoon of luster dust. Add the chains one at time, close the lid, and shake until the vine is covered evenly in gold. Repeat until all the licorice chains are coated. Add more luster dust as needed.

TO MAKE THE COOKIES: Line three baking sheets with silicone baking mats or parchment paper. Roll out the dough as directed and cut out in sets: one heart, one round, and three flowers each.

Place the hearts on one of the prepared baking sheets. Under the top of each heart, place the wide part of a wooden chopstick and gently press the dough around it. This will create the channel for the candy "chain" to be placed. Bake for 9 to 12 minutes or until just starting to brown. Allow to cool without moving for at least 20 minutes. Remove the chopsticks and discard. Bake the circles and flowers, on the second prepared baking sheet, for 9 to 12 minutes or until just starting to brown.

TO DECORATE: Color a small amount of icing (about ½ cup) yellow, and place into a pastry bag with a writing tip. Color about two-thirds of the remaining icing red, and store in an airtight container until needed. Use a pastry bag with a writing tip and some white icing to outline the round cookies. Use more white icing to flood the round cookies and allow to dry completely, at least 1 hour. Once dry, use the edible marker to draw the clock face onto each round

✦✦✦ Tips ✦✦✦

✦ The completed hearts with the chain and flowers are delicate. If you need to store before serving, consider adding the flowers up to 3 hours ahead. Store the hearts with the attached chain and clock face in a single layer in an airtight container for up to 5 days. Store the flowers in a separate airtight container.

✦ For an easier project, create flat heart cookies as normal and only attach the clock faces.

and set aside. Use the yellow icing to decorate each flower and cover with the white sanding sugar. Pipe a yellow center into each flower and allow to dry completely, at least 1 hour. While the cookies are drying, brush each candy vine with the gold luster dust, coating completely (see note).

TO ASSEMBLE: Place the heart cookies upside down on a silicone baking mat with the channel facing you. Fill the channel with red icing and press about 2 inches of the end of the candy vine into the channel, leaving the rest loose. Cover the vine with more icing and smooth slightly with an offset spatula. Outline and flood the rest of the heart with red icing, taking care not to overfill. Gently place a round clock face cookie in the center and leave undisturbed for at least 2 hours or until completely dry.

Add details by piping around the clock face with yellow icing and coating in gold sanding sugar, adding gold dragées to the connection between the "chain" and the heart to create a fob, and brush the red heart lightly with gold luster dust. "Glue" the flowers, three each, up the length of the chain with white icing.

Liquid Courage

Yield: 2 to 4 servings; 1 cup ginger syrup | GF, V, V+*

The Cowardly Lion gets his badge for courage from the Wizard of Oz, but he might appreciate another boost in liquid form—this time from iced green tea. Homemade ginger syrup offers an extra kick, with honey and your own apple shrub from the Apple Shrub Mocktini (page 95) adding sweetness—just like the lion himself. Pour into chilled glasses and toast to wishes granted and dreams come true.

FOR THE GINGER SYRUP:

4 ounces fresh ginger root, peeled and chopped into 1-inch pieces (about 1 cup)

1 cup water

1 cup sugar

FOR THE LIQUID COURAGE:

2 cups water

3 green tea bags

1 teaspoon honey

1 teaspoon vanilla extract

½ cup lemon juice

¼ cup apple shrub (page 95) or 2 tablespoons apple cider vinegar

Rosemary sprigs, for garnish

Note

This recipe is easily made vegan by replacing the honey with agave or maple syrup.

TO MAKE THE GINGER SYRUP: In a medium saucepan over medium-high heat, add the ginger, water, and sugar and stir until the sugar is dissolved. Reduce the heat to medium-low and simmer for 8 to 10 minutes, stirring occasionally. Cover and set aside in a cool place for 12 to 24 hours. Strain through a fine-mesh sieve, removing the ginger, pressing down gently to remove as much liquid as possible. Store refrigerated in a bottle or jar for up to 3 weeks.

TO MAKE THE LIQUID COURAGE: Using a saucepan or kettle over high heat, bring the water to a boil. Place the tea bags into a 1-quart measuring cup and pour the boiling water over them. Steep for 5 minutes. Remove the tea bags, stir in the honey to taste, and allow the tea to cool. In a large pitcher, combine the tea, vanilla, lemon juice, shrub or apple cider vinegar, and vanilla. Add 4 tablespoons of the ginger simple syrup, or to taste. If you feel there is enough ginger but it is not quite sweet enough, you can add more honey. Stir well, cover with a lid or plastic wrap, and refrigerate until ready to use, up to 24 hours. Stir again before serving and add, or pour over, ice. Garnish with fresh rosemary sprigs.

Magic Granita Slushy

Yield: 4 servings | GF, V, V+

Dorothy and her friends experience a magical entrance into the Wizard of Oz's castle, riding and singing in the carriage behind the Horse of a Different Color. Capture some of that color-changing magic in dessert form with this citrusy slushy. Adding blue butterfly pea syrup just before serving transforms the lemon-yellow ice into a gorgeous pink in front of your tasters' eyes.

FOR THE CITRUS GRANITA:

Zest of 2 lemons

Zest of 2 limes

½ cup fresh squeezed lemon juice (about 2 lemons)

½ cup fresh squeezed lime juice (about 3 limes)

2 cups boiling water

1 cup sugar

FOR THE COLOR-CHANGING SYRUP:

½ cup boiling water

¼ cup sugar

¼ teaspoon butterfly pea flower powder

Large sprig of mint, leaves removed and gently bruised

FOR SERVING:

Lime wedge

2 tablespoons purple confetti sugar (optional)

12 ounces sparkling water

TO MAKE THE CITRUS GRANITA: In a small bowl or measuring cup, stir the lemon zest, lime zest, lemon juice, and lime juice together.

Pour the boiling water into a heatproof bowl or measuring cup, add the sugar, and stir until completely clear. Stir the citrus mixture into the sugar mixture.

Pour the mixture into a shallow dish and place in the freezer. Every 30 minutes, use a fork to scrape the ice crystals from the bottom and the sides until all the liquid has become crystallized. Transfer to an airtight container and store in the freezer until ready to serve.

TO MAKE THE COLOR-CHANGING SYRUP: Add the boiling water to a heatproof measuring cup or bowl. Add the sugar and stir until completely clear. Add the butterfly pea flower powder and whisk until completely combined.

Add the mint leaves and stir until submerged. Allow to steep for 30 minutes. Strain into an airtight container, discarding the mint leaves, and refrigerate the syrup until ready to serve.

WHEN READY TO SERVE: Prepare four glasses by running a lime wedge around the rim and coating in the confetti sugar. Add either tall straws or spoons. Place 3 scoops of granita into each glass, about 1½ cups, and drizzle with about 2 tablespoons of syrup. Top with about 3 ounces of fizzy water.

Pull the Curtain Away Stuffed Wizard Rolls *

Yield: About 16 rolls | GF

Everything is not as it seems, as Dorothy and her friends learn during that fateful moment when Toto tugs back the curtain to reveal the Wizard of Oz. This recipe captures that sentiment on the plate. Instead of the classic cabbage, we've used chard to hold the beef and rice filling. Simmer the rolls in a tangy tomato sauce, then cloak them in more chard to create the "curtains" that mask your creation. No magic required here.

FOR THE TOMATO SAUCE:

2 tablespoons olive oil

1 small yellow onion, finely chopped

2 cloves garlic, finely minced

One 28-ounce can crushed tomatoes

2 tablespoons apple cider or red wine vinegar

¼ cup brown sugar

1 teaspoon kosher salt

½ teaspoon ground pepper

FOR THE FILLING:

½ cup long-grain rice, cooked

1 pound ground beef

1 small onion, finely diced

2 cloves garlic, finely minced

1 teaspoon fresh thyme leaves, chopped

2 tablespoons chopped fresh parsley or 1 tablespoon dried

1 teaspoon kosher salt

½ teaspoon ground pepper

1 egg, beaten

FOR THE STUFFED WIZARD ROLLS:

3 bunches Swiss chard

TO MAKE THE TOMATO SAUCE: In a large saucepan over medium heat, heat the olive oil. Add the onion and garlic and cook for about 10 minutes, stirring often, until the onion is translucent. Add the tomatoes, vinegar, brown sugar, salt, and pepper. Bring to a boil, then reduce the heat to medium-low. Simmer uncovered for 20 minutes, stirring occasionally.

TO MAKE THE FILLING: In a large bowl, combine the rice, beef, onion, garlic, thyme, parsley, salt, and pepper. Add the egg and gently mix the ingredients together until they are just incorporated. Do not overmix, which will make the meat tough as it cooks.

TO MAKE THE STUFFED WIZARD ROLLS: Bring a large pot of water to a boil over high heat. Rinse each chard leaf well. Cut off the stems at the base of each leaf. Blanch the chard leaves for 20 to 30 seconds. Drain and plunge into ice water to stop the cooking and preserve the color. Drain well.

Preheat the oven to 350°F. Spoon a thin layer of the sauce into a Dutch oven or 9-by-13-inch casserole dish. Working with one chard leaf at a time, lay it out flat on a cutting board. Using a sharp knife, cut the tough center rib out of the bottom third of the stem end in the shape of a narrow inverted V. Depending on the size of each leaf, place about 2 tablespoons of filling into the lower third of the leaf, forming an oval. Fold the bottom edge of the leaf over the filling and roll tightly, tucking in the sides. Place seam-side down into the prepared baking dish. Repeat until you have used all the filling. Wrap any remaining leaves and refrigerate to use later to make the "curtain."

Spoon the remaining sauce over the rolls. Cover the dish with a heavy lid or aluminum foil and bake for 1 hour. Remove and allow to rest for 5 minutes. Being careful not to burn yourself, gently stretch out each of the reserved chard leaves and arrange them stem-side up, allowing them to drape down over the rolls like a curtain. Arrange any smaller pieces on the top to create a valance over the stems. To serve, pull the "curtain" back to reveal the Stuffed Wizard Rolls.

Up High Picnic Pie

Yield: 8 to 12 servings

Sailing away on a hot-air balloon, perhaps? Take this classic picnic pie along for a snack. True to its name, a picnic pie is meant to be eaten cold—a perfect choice for your adventure. The Wizard of Oz may want to bring this pastry-encased delicacy with him as he sails up, up, and away from the Emerald City. It's even decorated with little hot-air balloons, in homage to the great and charming charlatan himself.

FOR THE PICNIC PIE:

1 whole chicken (about 3 pounds), cut into pieces

2 cups chicken broth (bone broth preferred; see note)

4 tablespoons olive oil, divided

2 large fennel bulbs, thinly sliced

2 small yellow onions, diced

1 teaspoon kosher salt, divided

One 15-ounce can cannellini beans, rinsed

½ pound white button, cremini, or baby bella mushrooms, sliced

2 cloves garlic, crushed

½ teaspoon freshly ground black pepper

1 teaspoon chopped fresh thyme leaves

1½ cups freshly grated Parmesan cheese (about 3 ounces)

FOR THE PASTRY:

4 cups all-purpose flour, plus more for dusting

¾ cup water

½ cup vegetable shortening

4 tablespoons salted butter, plus more for greasing the pan

½ cup milk

Food coloring (see note)

TO MAKE THE PICNIC PIE: Arrange the chicken pieces in the bottom of a Dutch oven or heavy stockpot. Pour the broth over the chicken and bring to a boil over medium heat. Once it comes to a boil, lower the heat immediately to medium-low and keep at a slow, gentle simmer. Partially cover the pot and cook for 45 to 60 minutes, or until the meat falls off the bones, turning the pieces at least once during the cooking process. Using tongs or a slotted spoon, remove the chicken and place onto a baking sheet. Strain the reinforced broth into a bowl using a fine-mesh strainer.

Using the same pot or Dutch oven, heat 2 tablespoons of olive oil over medium heat. Add the fennel, onions, and ½ teaspoon of salt, and sauté until soft, stirring occasionally, about 10 minutes. Add the reinforced broth and beans. Cover the pan, reduce the heat to medium-low, and cook for 15 minutes. Remove the lid and, stirring occasionally, cook for an additional 15 minutes. Set aside to cool for 30 minutes.

While the fennel mixture is cooling, heat the remaining 2 tablespoons of olive oil in a large skillet over medium heat. Add the sliced mushrooms and garlic, spreading them out into one layer. Without stirring, allow the mushrooms to cook until browned on one side, about 5 minutes. Stir once and cook for another 5 minutes. Sprinkle with ¼ teaspoon of salt and the pepper.

TO MAKE THE PASTRY: Add the flour to a large bowl and make a well in the center. In a small saucepan over medium-high heat, add the water, shortening, and butter. Stir until all the shortening and butter are melted and the mixture begins to boil. Add the mixture to the well in the flour and use a wooden spoon to stir it until it is cool enough to handle, about 2 to 3 minutes. Knead the mixture by hand a bit until all the ingredients are incorporated.

Remove two-thirds of the dough to a lightly floured surface, covering the remaining dough with a tea towel, and roll it out to about ¼-inch thickness. Gently lift the dough into a springform pan, making sure it goes all the way to the bottom and is pressed against the sides. If any tears occur, patch them by pressing the dough back together or adding some scraps to fill them in. Trim the edges so that there is about a ½-inch overhang all the way around the edges of the springform pan.

TO ASSEMBLE: Preheat the oven to 375°F.

Once cool enough to handle, separate the chicken meat from the bones, discarding the skin and bones. Add the chicken to the fennel mixture and fold, using a rubber spatula, until incorporated. Add the thyme and Parmesan cheese, mixing well. Add more salt and pepper to taste as needed (see note). Layer half of the chicken mixture into the pastry-lined springform pan. Arrange the mushrooms over the chicken mixture. Repeat with another layer of the chicken until you reach the top of the pastry lined springform pan. Press down gently with a spatula to eliminate any air pockets.

Work the scraps and the remaining dough back together and roll out until about ¼ inch thick to make an 8-inch top. Using a pastry brush, brush the edges of the crust with milk and lay the top crust over the filling. Fold in the pastry overhang and crimp the two pieces together, making sure they seal well. Roll out the scraps and cut out your decor, including a hot-air balloon, some clouds, and Toto, etc. Separate out the remaining milk into small bowls, add coloring, and, using a clean pastry brush or small craft brush (only used for food), paint your decor pieces. Paint the "background" of the top as desired and add the decor pieces. Make sure that the entire top piece and all the decor get brushed with milk.

Bake for 50 minutes. Remove from the oven, keeping the oven on. Allow the pie to rest for 5 minutes while placing a baking sheet into the oven. After 5 minutes, remove the baking sheet. Place the pie on the hot baking sheet and carefully remove the sides of the springform pan. Brush more milk on the top and sides of the pie. Bake for another 15 to 20 minutes, or until the sides are golden brown. Place onto a wire rack and allow to cool for 20 minutes if eating warm, or cool it completely if chilling to eat cold.

Carefully transfer the pie from the base of the springform pan to a serving plate. If planning to serve cold in traditional picnic pie style, wrap in parchment paper and then foil and refrigerate for at least 4 hours or up to 3 days.

There's No Place Like Home(made) Apple Pie

Yield: 8 servings | V

Imagine opening your eyes after a whirlwind trip to a magical land and finding yourself on your very own bed, with your family around you—and a piece of this juicy, crumbly apple pie. An easy oatmeal streusel topping saves you the trouble of cutting and fitting a top crust, with Granny Smith apples providing a tart contrast. It's Kansas farmyard homeyness in a pie pan—and in your stomach.

FOR THE OATMEAL CRUMBLE TOPPING:

½ cup all-purpose flour

½ cup brown sugar

½ cup oats

1 teaspoon ground cinnamon

¼ teaspoon ground nutmeg

½ teaspoon kosher salt

4 tablespoons cold unsalted butter, cut into small pieces

FOR THE PIE:

½ recipe Tried and True Pie Crust (page 22)

3 pounds Granny Smith apples, peeled, cored, and thinly sliced (about 6 or 7 apples)

Juice from 1 lemon

½ cup granulated sugar

½ cup brown sugar

2 teaspoons ground cinnamon

1 teaspoon kosher salt

¼ cup unsalted butter

3 tablespoons all-purpose flour

1 teaspoon vanilla extract

1 egg, separated

1 teaspoon water

TO MAKE THE OATMEAL CRUMBLE TOPPING: In a small bowl, mix the flour, brown sugar, oats, cinnamon, nutmeg, and salt. Add the butter and cut it into the flour mixture using a pastry cutter or two forks until it forms pea-size crumbles. Refrigerate, covered, if not using immediately.

TO MAKE THE PIE: Make the crust and place in the refrigerator while you make the filling.

In a large bowl, combine the apples, lemon juice, granulated sugar, brown sugar, cinnamon, and salt. Let sit for 20 minutes. Preheat the oven to 350°F.

Roll the dough into an ⅛-inch-thick circle that is 4 inches larger than the diameter of a pie plate. Fold it into quarters and place into the pie plate. Unfold and gently press the dough into the plate. Trim the crust leaving a ½-inch overhang. To make a fluted edge, use the index finger of your dominant hand to press out along the edge, from the inside of the pie. Use your thumb and index finger of your other hand to pinch around the dominant finger from the outside. Continue around the entire edge. Place the pie plate in the freezer while you finish the filling and make the topping.

Place a colander over another bowl and drain the apples, reserving the liquid.

In a medium saucepan over medium heat, heat the butter. Whisking constantly, add the flour and cook for 1 minute. Whisk in the reserved apple liquid and the vanilla. Whisking constantly, cook until the mixture begins to come off the sides, 2 to 3 minutes. Remove from the heat and set aside to cool for 10 minutes. Stir the slightly cooled flour mixture into the apples until well coated and any remaining juices have been incorporated.

In a small bowl, using a fork, beat the egg white well. Remove the prepared crust from the freezer and brush the bottom and sides with the egg white. Add the yolk and water to the remaining egg white and beat together with the fork and use to brush the edge of the piecrust. Place the apple mixture into the crust, filling until just below the start of the crimped edge. Sprinkle the topping evenly over the apples and press down slightly. Place on a baking sheet to catch any drippings and bake for 50 to 60 minutes, or until deep golden brown. Allow to sit for at least 1 hour before serving.

Conclusion

You've journeyed into the Land of Oz, clicked your heels, and now you're home, perhaps opening your eyes in your farmhouse bedroom in Kansas, or perhaps standing at your own kitchen counter, leafing through the recipes that have taken you over the rainbow and back.

You've traveled from crullers and rolls to lollipops to cheese bricks, spicy lemonade, and green quiches—then all the way back to homey apple pie. And perhaps you've learned a bit, too—about how to create an apple from pastry dough, construct a Bacon-Wrapped Date Winged Monkey on a stick (page 117), and, miraculously, make your own marshmallows (page 73).

Dorothy's world offers color and fun, strange whimsy, and a good scare. Now you've captured some of those things, too, in edible form. Whether you're serving cold Twister Shakes (page 37) on your front porch or dishing up Field of Corn Polenta (page 84), we hope you'll invite your friends to your table as well. Dorothy learned the sweetness of home and the joy of friendship while she was in the Land of Oz. Your kitchen will be that sweet place now, too, with people you love to share it with.

Dietary Considerations ★

<table>
<tr><td>**GF**: Gluten-Free</td><td>**V***: Easily Made Vegetarian</td></tr>
<tr><td>**GF***: Easily Made Gluten-Free</td><td>**V+**: Vegan</td></tr>
<tr><td>**V**: Vegetarian</td><td>**V+***: Easily Made Vegan</td></tr>
</table>

CHAPTER 1: KANSAS: AUNTIE EM'S RECIPE BOX

Auntie Em's Crullers: **V**

Always on Hand Cake: **V**

Dinner on the Farm Rolls: **V**

Auntie Em's Prize-Winning Pulled Pork Cinnamon Roll

Peach Iced Tea: **GF, V, V+**

Cake Truffle Eggs: **V**

Tried and True Pie Crust: **V**

Toto Shortbread Cookies: **V**

Pull Up to the Table Bacon Cheddar Biscuits

Pull Me Out of the Pen Pork, Kansas Style: **GF**

Old-Fashioned Lemonade: **GF, V, V+**

Grilled Sausages with Marvelous Campfire Spread: **GF***

Professor Marvel's Crystal Ball Cookies: **V**

Farmhand Egg Sandwiches

Where Will It Land? Twister Cupcakes: **V**

Twister Shakes: **GF*, V**

CHAPTER 2: OVER THE RAINBOW

Over the Rainbow Crepe Cake: **GF*, V**

Savory Sweet Potato Tartlets: **V, V+***

Rainbow Crudités and Hummus: **GF, V, V+**

Savory Pinwheel Lollipops

Glittery Glinda Cake: **V**

Good Witch Pink Lemonade: **GF, V, V+**

Ruby-Red Punch: **GF, V, V+**

Ding-Dong Graham Cracker House: **V**

Festive Munchkin Goodwitches: **V***

Flower Pot Cupcakes with Rice Paper Flowers: **V**

Glinda Strawberry Jasmine Bubble Tea: **GF, V, V+***

Cordial Munchkin Sweetness: **GF, V, V+**

Lollipop Guild Meringues: **GF*, V**

Blueberry Basil Marshmallow Bluebirds: **GF**

Ruby Slipper Cupcakes: **V**

"We're Not in Kansas Anymore" Fruit and Edible
   Flower Board: **GF, V, V+***

CHAPTER 3: FOLLOW THE YELLOW BRICK ROAD

Follow the Spiral Omelet: **GF, V**

Field of Corn Polenta Bar: **GF, V, V+***

Cornstalk Cheese Straws: **V**

Oh, Look! Apples and Walnut Salad with
   Shrub Vinaigrette: **GF, V*, V+***

"She Was Hungry" Baked Apples: **V**

Lions and Tigers and Bear Claws, Oh My!: **V**

Apple Shrub Mocktini: **GF, V, V+**

Oil Me Salad Dressing: **GF, V, V+***

If I Only Had a Heart-Shaped Ravioli: **V***

Smart Cookies: **GF, V**

I'm Losing My Hay: **GF*, V, V+**

Cowardly Cupcakes: **V**

I'm Feeling Chicken Liver Pate: **GF**

Field of Poppies Focaccia Bread: **V***

Poppy Macarons: **V, GF**

Mountain Climber: **GF, V, V+**

CHAPTER 4: THE WICKED CASTLE

Bacon-Wrapped Date Winged Monkeys: **GF**

Monkey Goes Bananas: **GF, V, V+***

Wicked Lemonade: **GF, V, V+**

My Pretty Wicked Mole with Green Polenta: **GF**

What a World Sphere: **GF*, V**

Wicked *Cruel*-lers: **V**

Fiery Crackers: **V, V+***

Wicked Black Bread: **V, V+**

Badwitches: **V**

Wicked Crystal Ball Shaker Cookies: **V**

"I'm Melting" Matcha Ice Cream with Hat Topper: **GF*, V**

Savory Wicked Crepe Cake: **V**

Wicked Hummus: **GF, V, V+***

CHAPTER 5: EMERALD CITY

Emerald City Quiche: **GF*, V**

Emerald City Salad with Creamy Green
   Goddess Dressing: **GF, V*, V+***

Emerald City Pistachio Cake with Glass Pears: **GF, V**

Honor Rolls

A Pie of a Different Color: **V**

Fuzzy Mitten: **GF, V, V+***

Be Still, My Ticking Heart Cookies: **V**

Liquid Courage: **GF, V, V+***

Magic Granita Slushy: **GF, V, V+**

Pull the Curtain Away Stuffed Wizard Rolls: **GF**

Up High Picnic Pie

There's No Place Like Home(made) Apple Pie: **V**

Recipes Organized by Type

BREAKFASTS
Auntie Em's Crullers
Auntie Em's Prize-Winning Pulled Pork Cinnamon Roll
Farmhand Egg Sandwiches
Follow the Spiral Omelet
Lions and Tigers and Bear Claws, Oh My!
I'm Losing My Hay
Wicked *Cruel*-lers

APPETIZERS/SIDES
Dinner on the Farm Rolls
Pull Up to the Table Bacon Cheddar Biscuits
Savory Sweet Potato Tartlets
Rainbow Crudités and Hummus
"We're Not in Kansas Anymore" Fruit and Edible Flower Board
Field of Corn Polenta Bar
Cornstalk Cheese Straws
Oil Me Salad Dressing
Field of Poppies Focaccia Bread
Bacon-Wrapped Date Winged Monkeys
Fiery Crackers
Wicked Black Bread
Wicked Hummus

MAINS
Pull Me Out of the Pen Pork, Kansas Style
Grilled Sausages with Marvelous Campfire Spread
Savory Pinwheel Lollipops
Festive Munchkin Goodwitches
Oh, Look! Apples and Walnut Salad with Shrub Vinaigrette
If I Only Had a Heart-Shaped Ravioli
I'm Feeling Chicken Liver Pâté
My Pretty Wicked Mole with Green Polenta
Badwitches
Savory Wicked Crepe Cake
Emerald City Quiche
Emerald City Salad with Creamy Green Goddess Dressing
Honor Rolls
Pull the Curtain Away Stuffed Wizard Rolls
Up High Picnic Pie

DESSERTS
Always on Hand Cake
Cake Truffle Eggs
Tried and True Pie Crust
Toto Shortbread Cookies
Professor Marvel's Crystal Ball Cookies
Where Will It Land? Twister Cupcakes
Over the Rainbow Crepe Cake
Glittery Glinda Cake

Ding-Dong Graham Cracker House
Flower Pot Cupcakes with Rice Paper Flowers
Lollipop Guild Meringues
Blueberry Basil Marshmallow Bluebirds
Ruby Slipper Cupcakes
"She Was Hungry" Baked Apples
Smart Cookies!
Cowardly Cupcakes
Poppy Macarons
What a World Sphere
Wicked Crystal Ball Shaker Cookies
"I'm Melting" Matcha Ice Cream with Hat Topper
Emerald City Pistachio Cake with Glass Pears
A Pie of a Different Color
Be Still, My Ticking Heart Cookies
There's No Place Like Home(made) Apple Pie

DRINKS
Peach Iced Tea
Old-Fashioned Lemonade
Twister Shakes
Good Witch Pink Lemonade
Ruby-Red Punch
Glinda Strawberry Jasmine Bubble Tea
Cordial Munchkin Sweetness
Apple Shrub Mocktini
Mountain Climber
Monkey Goes Bananas
Wicked Lemonade
Fuzzy Mitten
Liquid Courage
Magic Granita Slushy

Conversion Charts

KITCHEN MEASUREMENTS

CUPS	TABLESPOONS	TEASPOONS	FLUID OUNCES
¹⁄₁₆ cup	1 Tbsp	3 tsp	½ fl oz
⅛ cup	2 Tbsp	6 tsp	1 fl oz
¼ cup	4 Tbsp	12 tsp	2 fl oz
⅓ cup	5½ Tbsp	16 tsp	2⅔ fl oz
½ cup	8 Tbsp	24 tsp	4 fl oz
⅔ cup	10⅔ Tbsp	32 tsp	5⅓ fl oz
¾ cup	12 Tbsp	36 tsp	6 fl oz
1 cup	16 Tbsp	48 tsp	8 fl oz

LENGTH

IMPERIAL	METRIC
1 in	2.5 cm
2 in	5 cm
4 in	10 cm
6 in	15 cm
8 in	20 cm
10 in	25 cm
12 in	30 cm

OVEN TEMPERATURES

FAHRENHEIT	CELSIUS
200°F	93°C
225°F	107°C
250°F	121°C
275°F	135°C
300°F	149°C
325°F	163°C
350°F	177°C
375°F	191°C
400°F	204°C
425°F	218°C
450°F	232°C

⭐ Fry Station Safety Tips

If you're making something that requires deep frying, here are some important tips to prevent any kitchen fires:

✦ If you don't have a dedicated deep fryer, use a Dutch oven or a high-walled sauté pan.

✦ Never have too much oil in the pan! You don't want hot oil spilling out as soon as you put the food in.

✦ Only use a suitable cooking oil, like canola, peanut, or vegetable oil.

✦ Always keep track of the oil temperature with a thermometer—350°F to 375°F should do the trick.

✦ Never put too much food in the pan at the same time!

✦ Never put wet food in the pan. It will splatter and may cause burns.

✦ Always have a lid nearby to cover the pan in case it starts to spill over or catch fire. A properly rated fire extinguisher is also great to have on hand in case of emergencies.

✦ Never leave the pan unattended and never let children near the pan.

✦ Never, ever touch the hot oil directly.

Glossary

Biscuit cutter: Although cookie cutters, mason jars, a glass, or bench scraper will work, biscuit cutters are sharper, which helps cut through the dough without twisting, making sure you get the best height for your biscuits.

Black cocoa powder: Used to give the Oil Me Salad Dressing (page 97) its characteristic appearance, black cocoa powder is used to add dark color and unsweetened chocolate flavor to the Savory Wicked Crepe Cake (page 139), Wicked Black Bread (page 130), My Pretty Wicked Mole with Green Polenta (page 122), Wicked *Cruel*-lers (page 127), and Wicked Crystal Ball Shaker Cookies (page 134).

Black garlic: Available in Asian markets or online, black garlic is aged garlic with a chewy texture and a molasses-like flavor. It adds softer garlic notes to the black hummus (page 141), purple hummus (page 44), and the mole (page 122).

Black sesame seeds: Available in Asian markets or online, black sesame seeds add both color and a nuttier flavor to the black hummus (page 141).

Butterfly pea flowers: These dried flower blossoms are commonly used in herbal tea drinks. When added to a recipe, they provide a beautiful deep blue color. If combined with acids, like lemon juice, the color turns to pink or purple. They are available online and in some health food stores. They are also turned into a powder and an extract.

Cake strips: Cake strips are heat-proof strips, made from a similar material to pot holders, that help cakes bake very level. The strips shield the edge of the cake so it bakes more slowly, preventing the center from "volcanoing" up.

Candy thermometer: Sometimes called fry thermometers, these long glass thermometers can be clipped to the side of a pot. They can withstand temperatures of at least 500°F and are used to measure the temperatures of frying oil or sugar when making syrups, candies, and certain frostings.

Cutting in butter: To work cold butter into dry ingredients until it is broken down into small pea-size pieces and dispersed evenly throughout the mixture. It is important that the butter is very cold so it does not begin to soften. These little pieces of butter, surrounded by the dry ingredients, are what create the flakiness in pastry.

Dried rose petals: Made from either store-bought or home-dried (pesticide-free) rose petals, use them to garnish the rim of your Ruby-Red Punch (page 55) or sprinkle petals or buds around your "We're Not in Kansas Anymore" Fruit and Edible Flower Board (page 79).

Dry measuring cups: Measuring tools that usually come in sets of ¼ cup, ⅓ cup, ½ cup, and 1 cup. They are ideal for measuring dry ingredients such as flour, sugar, rice, and pasta.

Dutch oven: A large (usually 5- to 6-quart), heavy cooking pot ideal for making stews, braises, and deep-fried foods. Dutch ovens are often made from cast iron or enameled cast iron, which makes them hold and distribute heat evenly. A Dutch oven works well when cooking with both high and low temperatures, making it a versatile vessel and handy addition to every kitchen.

Edible flowers: Used for making the ice cubes in Good Witch Pink Lemonade (page 53) and to decorate the "We're Not in Kansas Anymore" Fruit and Edible Flower Board (page 79). Making sure no pesticides have been used, edible flowers can be homegrown or found in your produce aisle. Flowers to look for are zucchini blossoms, roses, pansies, chive blossoms, marigolds, lavender, violets, and nasturtiums.

Egg wash: A mixture used to create a sheen or gloss on breads, pastries, and other baked goods. Whisk together 1 egg and 1 tablespoon of water until light and foamy. Use a pastry brush to apply before baking when the recipe requires.

Folding in: This refers to gently adding an ingredient with a spatula in wide, gentle strokes. Do not whisk or stir vigorously. Folding allows any airiness already established to stay intact.

Freeze-dried fruits: Freeze-dried fruits give you great natural color and flavor when making dips for your fruit board. You can replace them with fresh or frozen fruits, but they will add more liquid, so it is best to stick with Greek yogurt if using fresh or frozen fruits.

Granulated sugar: A highly refined sugar made from sugarcane or beets that is known for its white color and fine texture. All of the molasses has been removed from this type of sugar.

Greasing a pan: Coating a pan with nonstick cooking spray, oil, softened butter, or shortening to keep (usually) baked goods, such as cakes, from sticking.

High-heat vs. nonstick pans: A high-heat pan—as its name suggests—can stand up to high-heat cooking, generally temperatures between 400°F and 600°F. They're usually made of stainless steel, cast iron, or enameled cast iron and can be used on the stovetop or oven—if the handle is made of an ovenproof material. Nonstick cookware contains a coating that helps keep foods from sticking (particularly eggs), but they can't be used at the same temperatures as high-heat pans. If you are cooking with nonstick cookware, make sure you know the manufacturer's heat limits for your cookware. Most nonstick cookware should not be used at above medium heat on a stovetop (about 350°F) and is not generally suitable for the oven.

Immersion blender: A handheld machine used for puréeing soups and sauces in the pot.

Isomalt: Isomalt is a type of sugar that is very easy to work with for sugar decorations. Cooked isomalt pieces don't need to be cooked with a candy thermometer to a hard crack stage. Once melted, poured, and re-hardened, they are shiny, hard, and don't pick up as much moisture as regular sugar. Isomalt can be colored and flavored easily. It is available at specialty baking stores, craft stores with baking aisles, or online.

Liquid measuring cup: Clear glass or plastic measuring tools used for measuring precise amounts of liquids by lining up the level of liquid to the marks on the cup. Useful sizes include 1 cup, 2 cup, and 4 cup.

Luster dust and petal dust: Both luster and petal dust are food-safe colorants that can be brushed onto food dry or combined with very small amounts of clear alcohol, such as vodka, to create paints. Luster dust has a lot of sparkle, whereas petal dust tends to be matte. Both are available at specialty baking stores, craft stores with baking aisles, or online.

Macaronage: The process of combining meringue with an almond mixture. You need to fold the two mixtures together by pulling a spatula through the mixture and then around the bowl, pulling the rest of the mixture toward the middle. The final texture, for the bottom macaron, should flow like a thick batter. In order to create the "textured" poppy-shaped macaron (page 110), the batter must be under-*macaronaged*.

Milk: Unless otherwise noted, these recipes call for dairy milk. In most cases, any percentage of milk fat will do, unless otherwise noted.

Muddle: A short-handled tool that is textured on one end and used to mash together ingredients such as fruits, herbs, and sugar when making flavored drinks.

Packed brown sugar: When baking, and in most other recipes, when you measure brown sugar, it needs to be packed in the measuring cup. Brown sugar is sticky and does not naturally compact together. As you fill the measuring cup, press down gently with the back of a spoon or your fingers until you have a flat surface, then continue to add brown sugar until the cup is full.

Parchment paper: Food-safe paper that can withstand temperatures of up to 450°F—even up to 500°F for short baking times—that's used to line pans for baking and roasting. Parchment paper keeps foods from sticking and makes cleanup easier.

Peeling ginger: To peel fresh ginger root, use the edge of a small spoon to scrape away the peel. This keeps the root intact, with less waste, and allows you to easily navigate the lumps and bumps.

Piping frosting: The process of decorating cakes and cookies by squeezing frosting placed in a decorating bag over them. Piping can be done with or without a decorating tip—or even in a plastic bag with one corner snipped off to allow the frosting to be applied in a neat rope shape.

Purple sweet potato powder or ube powder: Delicious, nutritious, and vibrant, this ingredient is used to make hummus purple and purple Goodwitches (page 61).

Rose water: Rose water is used in cordial hibiscus syrup (page 69) and Glinda Strawberry Jasmine Bubble Tea (page 67). Made from rose petals, it brings a soft floral note to your recipes.

Royal icing: This icing is used for decorating cookies or creating decorations that will harden like candy. When whipped stiff, it can be piped into shapes or used to create outlines. It can also be thinned, with a bit of water, to a thick batter consistency and used to flood the surface of cookies, creating a smooth surface.

Salt: Unless otherwise noted, use your salt of choice in the recipes in this book. Kosher salt—which is coarser than regular table salt—is the type of salt that is most commonly used throughout the book.

Sear: To create a crust on a piece of meat, poultry, or fish by placing it in a very hot pan or on a very hot grill. The high heat quickly caramelizes the natural sugars in the food, creating a deeply browned and flavorful crust. Once the crust is formed, the heat is usually turned down so that the interior of the meat can cook properly before the outside is burned.

Sift: The process of putting flour, powdered sugar, or cornstarch through a fine-mesh sieve to aerate and remove lumps. Multiple ingredients—such as flour, salt, and leavenings—are often sifted together to blend them.

Silicone baking mat: Used to line shallow baking pans to prevent sticking when making foods such as cookies and pastries. They can withstand high temperatures in the oven and can also be used in the freezer. Dough can be rolled out on them, and they can easily go from prep station to chilling to the oven without having to move the dough. They are easy to clean and reusable.

Simmer: To cook a liquid, such as a sauce or soup, at low-enough heat so that bubbles are just barely breaking over the surface.

Turmeric: A spice found easily in your grocery store and is used to make yellow and green Goodwitch Rolls (page 61).

Vanilla paste vs. vanilla extract: Vanilla bean paste provides strong vanilla flavor and beautiful vanilla bean flecks without having to split and scrape a vanilla bean. Although it is more expensive than extract, there are situations in which it really elevates the finished dish. When that's the case, a recipe will specifically call for vanilla bean paste, but it can always be replaced in a 1-to-1 ratio with vanilla extract.

Whisk: A handled tool with thin wires arranged in various shapes used for mixing and whipping liquids and batters to combine ingredients or incorporate air into them. The two most common types of whisks are the balloon whisk, which has a bulbous end that narrows down toward the handle, and the sauce whisk, which has a round coil that sits flat on the bottom of the pan.

INSIGHT
EDITIONS

PO Box 3088
San Rafael, CA 94912
www.insighteditions.com

f Find us on Facebook: www.facebook.com/InsightEditions
📷 Follow us on Instagram: @insighteditions

ISBN: 979-8-88663-519-5

Publisher: Raoul Goff
VP, Group Publisher: Vanessa Lopez
VP, Creative: Chrissy Kwasnik
VP, Manufacturing: Alix Nicholaeff
Art Director: Stuart Smith
Designer: Leah Bloise Lauer
Senior Editor: Anna Wostenberg
Editorial Assistant: Alecsander Zapata
VP, Senior Executive Project Editor: Vicki Jaeger
Production Manager: Deena Hashem
Senior Production Manager, Subsidiary Rights: Lina s Palma-Temena

Art Director of Photography: Judy Wiatrek Trum
Photographer: Ted Thomas
Food and Prop Stylist: Elena P. Craig
Assistant Food Stylists: Patricia Parrish, Lauren Tedeschi

Insight Editions, in association with Roots of Peace, will plant two trees for each tree used in the manufacturing of this book. Roots of Peace is an internationally renowned humanitarian organization dedicated to eradicating land mines worldwide and converting war-torn lands into productive farms and wildlife habitats. Roots of Peace will plant two million fruit and nut trees in Afghanistan and provide farmers there with the skills and support necessary for sustainable land use.

Manufactured in China by Insight Editions

10 9 8 7 6 5 4 3 2 1